Wonderstruck

Other Books by Greg Wright

Tolkien in Perspective
Peter Jackson in Perspective
Two Roads Through Narnia
A Narnia Glossary of Obscure Terms
The Da Vinci Code Adventure
West of the Gospel
The Gospel of Doubt
What I Want for You

Wonderstruck by The Methow
Wonderstruck by Art & Artists

Wonderstruck

because the universe wants us to be in awe of what comes next

Greg Wright

Methow Press
Twisp, Washington 98856

© 2018-2025 by Greg Wright

Published by Methow Press
P.O. Box 1213, Twisp, WA 98856
www.methowpress.com

Printed in the United States of America

All rights reserved. No part of this publication may be reproduced, stored in a retrieval system, or transmitted in any form or by any means—for example, electronic, photocopy, or recording—without the prior written permission of the publisher. The only exception is brief quotations in printed reviews.

Essays in this work have appeared previously on Facebook and Medium.

ISBN: 979-8-9913567-2-5

Cover image courtesy NASA.

Unless otherwise noted, all Scripture quotations in this work are from The Holy Bible, New International Version ® NIV ® Copyright © 1973, 1978, 1984 by the International Bible Society. All rights reserved.

Extended quotes from books, songs, and poetry written by the author's friends and associates have been used by permission. Other quotes from works by public figures are used under Fair Use provisions of U.S. copyright law and are intended, as a form of scholarly critique, to draw attention to and praise the works of those public figures.

Contents

Introduction i	Foreign Agents 79
My Best Days 1	Fairies 87
Daybreak 4	Forgiveness 89
Wonderstruck 7	Wind 93
Ole and Trufa 12	Flaws 96
Silence 15	Affirmation 99
Jane Stephenson 17	Change 103
Christopher Hitchens 19	Revolutionary Love 105
The Moment 22	Joffrey Hooks 108
Beauty 25	Coffee Cake 111
Elissa Weisz 28	Clarence Jordan 114
Rusty Van Deusen 30	Middle English 117
Chris Chesser 32	Home 120
Chesterton 36	Timing 122
The Defendant 40	Lewis & Clark 125
Serendipity 44	Mushing 128
Butterfly 53	Scott Hicks 135
Backcountry 55	Gregory Boyle 139
Peter Alford 57	1 + 1 = 3 143
Disposable Cameras 59	Acceptance 145
Heaven Knows 62	The Road Taken 149
Prunella vulgaris 65	The Gutter 154
Brewminatti 68	Virtual Friends 160
Finding Home 70	The Infinite 164
The Walls 73	Perchance to Wake 168
Privilege 75	Joy 172

Destiny 175	Allegiance 233
The Millionaire Waltz 178	Democracy 239
Jon Kottwitz 180	Gifts 244
Coincidence 185	Unexpected Gifts 247
Brian Tittle 188	Work 250
Denise Driscoll 193	Panang 253
Patience 197	Loose Change 257
Michelle 200	Clarity 260
Bos 204	Boonie 266
Four Loves 209	Finding the Lost 269
Dream of Robin and Frog ... 215	A Hat 272
Experiencing God 218	Vivian 276
March 11, 2018 222	Coincidence? 280
Marriage 225	Valerie 285
Civil Discourse 229	Acknowledgements 291

Introduction

After my wife Jenn passed away at the end of 2017 in the wake of nearly fifteen years of terminal illness, I began writing a series of letters to her on a Facebook page titled "Memos to the Missus." The tagline was "Because who else would I tell?"

As the words began to flow more freely and expressively, and as I began to discover how much of life remained to me—and the flavor of that life—the Wonderstruck essays began in very modest form as Facebook Notes, a short-form essay layout mothballed by Facebook in 2020.

The first essay was an exceedingly short and simple reflection on my April 2018 raft trip through the Grand Canyon and a performance of Ferde Grofé's "Grand Canyon Suite" by the Auburn, Washington, Symphony—an unexpected treat as part of a musical program co-hosted by performance artist and friend Adrian Wyard.

But Wonderstruck grew rapidly from there. From the start, the essays have been both humanist and metaphysical, originating in a profound belief that life is not entirely random... and that the intention of the universal and infinite works itself out through the interactions that we have with one another and all the world around us.

The time is ripe for optimism. But then, the time is always ripe.

By way of metaphor, consider my fifteen years as a caregiver. When I was carrying Jenn piggyback to doctors' appointments in 2003 because she was too weak to manage stairs, I could not have anticipated that was merely the opening salvo of a prolonged and agonizing medical ordeal.

I could also not have guessed at the intense joy or wonder we would experience at times throughout that trial, or at the personal and spiritual growth which would result.

But the beginning of our story was infused with enough magic, and its end bathed in enough foreshadowing, that when it came to its close I had sufficient experience of the world and its workings to know that all was not lost.

The time was ripe, ripe for something. I just did not know what. To an extent, I was like a moon-eyed Tony in *West Side Story*. "The air is humming… and something great is coming!"

And something great did.

On a certain day and at a very certain time, as you will read, I discovered a word for that feeling. "Wonderstruck."

Everything that you read in these pages is 100% true, if much of it wildly improbable. I have lived my questions, as Rilke once recommended to a young poet, and these essays are a record of my progress, gradually, without perhaps even noticing it, toward living into my own answers.

I invite you to question my experience, to ponder whether such a universe can actually exist. You may find it hard to believe, as it may defy your own experience of the world.

But be patient with my words, *especially* if they resonate, and read them slowly. And also be patient with your own journey as you live your own questions.

∎

The essays in this collection are presented in the order in which they were first published, starting in April 2018, and focus on the philosophical and metaphysical underpinnings of the state of wonder.

Wonderstruck essays focused on the people and places of the Methow Valley have been collected under a separate cover, as have the Wonderstruck essays about art and artists.

Greg Wright
Winthrop, Washington
December 1, 2024

My Best Days

I finally let myself listen to Danny Gokey's album *My Best Days*.

It was one of my late wife's favorites, both inspiration for moving forward and a potent reminder that the end of Jenn's life was not that far away.

There's something about the way the album is structured, and the way that Gokey sings the songs, which walks a fine line between grief and hopefulness. On the hopeful side, the album starts off with the title track, "My Best Days Are Ahead of Me."

> There's a whole lot of world out there
> That I can't wait to see
> My best days are ahead of me

Jenn sang that song with a passion, and she really did have her best days ahead of her when a press copy of that album arrived in our mail in early 2010. She had her stomach removed that summer, and the years that followed were the best we had together.

> I don't know about you
> But I was put here to live and love
> So what if I don't do it like everybody else does
> They say I'm out on the edge
> I'm too willing to risk every bone every breath
> They say all I am is a crazy dream
> Like that's a bad thing

We lived the crazy dream for several years until Jenn's health started into its final decline.

> I don't really know what tomorrow will bring
> But I'm open to all possibilities
> Cause I still believe

Jenn did believe.

Mostly, Jenn agreed with Gokey's grandmother that moving forward requires "getting a little life on you." And she wept—well, *we* wept—every time Gokey sang the song that closes the album.

> I don't wanna feel better
> I don't wanna not remember
> I will always see your face
> In the shadows of this haunted place
> I will laugh, I will cry, shake my fist at the sky
> But I will not say goodbye

So it was about time I gave myself permission to listen. And weep if I needed to. Or not. It was just about time.

I was surprised to find that, in the months since I had last listened, the songs had become much more about me than about Jenn. Much more about my life moving forward than about her life ending.

And I was surprised to find that I did not weep. Because for some reason the songs helped me see the future more clearly than they reminded me of the past.

But this was not what floored me. No.

As I told my friend Peter about this over lunch, he said, "Well, you know, Greg, that makes sense." I asked why.

"Because Gokey wrote those songs not long after his own wife died."

I had no idea. Yeah, it all makes sense now.

■

Daybreak

Boy, was I depressed a year ago!

Out of the blue this morning, a college friend I haven't spoken to in thirty-four years contacted me on Messenger. We used to play in the same band—me on sax, she on piano—though I can't recall for sure if we played in that band at the same time. I think we did, though!

And I think one of the numbers we played together was a cover of Springsteen's "Sherry Darling." Just about a year ago, I wrote a pretty long piece about those years and about the impact that Springsteen's music had—and continues to have—on my life. In particular, I wrote about Clarence Clemons' sax solo in "Jungleland," the final track on *Born to Run*.

I concluded the piece with the following:

> The distance, I think, is what allowed "Jungleland" to hit me like a ton of bricks yesterday. That and life experience. Maturity, and loss.

> Seven of the eight tracks on the album exude a strange optimism in the face of adversity, a sort of stubborn determination that, yeah, life may stink–but as long as there's a car, a road, and some chance of romance there's light on the horizon.

But the album only begins on Mary's porch—and with that slamming screen door. It ends in the dark of Jungleland, and there's no hint of dawn.

"In a tunnel uptown, the Rat's own dream guns him down... No one watches as the ambulance pulls away... They just stand back and let it all be."

And you see, I know that's the end of the story even as Clarence Clemons hits the opening note of his signature tenor sax solo.

He hits it and holds it, like it's the last pure thing he'll ever play or hear. There's no rush to end it. No bravado, no flash, no trill. No virtuosic flair. Only the barest hint of vibrato as the interminable bars of the note wind down and he moves reluctantly on to whatever's next.

It's a simple acknowledgement that there's no escape, that there is no future for the Rat, nor for the Barefoot Girl.

There is only today, tonight, and that is all there will ever be.

"In the quick of a knife, they reach for their moment / And try to make an honest stand / But they wind up wounded, not even dead."

So I weep, and I wonder again at what Virginia felt that endless Saturday night long ago. Clarence, and my heart, still hold that note.

The dawn never comes. Just darkness. Darkness on the edge of town.

The thing about darkness, though, is that dawn sneaks up on you. Its approach is almost imperceptible, and you never know when it's coming.

I didn't realize it at the time, but the dawn started breaking on me last August—and its approach was so surprising, because there was still so much dying for Jenn to do... so much letting go left for the both of us.

Here's to the dawn breaking, anyway, and to the surprise of it all! To moving on to whatever's next...

■

Wonderstruck

I suppose I ought to explain that this whole "Wonderstruck" concept has been working its way into my brain for the last two months, the product of a long sequence of hyperventilation-inducing "almost scary" coincidences.

It started on March 11, 2017, really. I wrote a bit about that in my final "Memo to the Missus" the morning of March 12.

> Hello, Luv!
>
> Yesterday morning, I recorded the Harambee worship band performing two songs that will be included in your Celebration service, coming up quickly. It was good for you to have my full attention during the music. It was very cathartic, helping bring to a close a certain chapter of my life with you.
>
> After church, Peter and I made plans to meet at Coulon Park to hang out before I went to Elane's birthday celebration. I couldn't get parking at Coulon, so we changed plans to meet at the Cedar River Park by Carco Theater. After Peter agreed to the change via text, I of course got a parking spot at Coulon... but left anyway, since Peter was already on his way to Cedar River.
>
> Upon arriving there and sitting on the riverbeach steps to wait, I recalled that I had walked by those very steps exactly eight weeks earlier, January 14. That was the day of my six-

mile walk with Denise along the Cedar River trail, and the beginning of the problems with my knee, even though my heart was so light and full of joy that morning. What a special day that was, for many reasons.

As I was talking with Peter, and we were talking about how I might consider loving myself a bit better, it also dawned on me that the park bench not forty feet away was one of the secluded spots where you and I did much of our courting on cool springs nights exactly twenty years ago following rehearsals for *In the Presence of my Enemies*. What a strange, strange thing that I would have so much joy and so much sorrow attached to that one place... and that a failure to find a parking spot elsewhere should send me there on Sunday.

As I was typing this note this morning, I noticed that after literally years of preparing the space for habitation, birds are finally nesting in the hollowed-out fencepost outside out living-room window, the one where you snapped the photo of the mushroom. It's good to know that beautiful life can spring from pretty rotten stuff!

With lots of love,

Hublet.

A good deal more than I wrote also happened on March 11, the type of bizarre synchronicity that makes you shake your head in bafflement. It was the beginning of a major awakening of my own.

Yes, "It's good to know that beautiful life can spring from pretty rotten stuff!"

I also have not yet written of what ensued after publishing that note the morning of March 12. Suffice to say for now that the day ended with me on the phone with my old friend John Adami declaring, "I'm not sure what you have to tell me, John, but based on the last 48 hours of my life I can bet that you are going to say at least one thing that will intersect with my life in a way that is beyond mere coincidence." And I was able to tell him exactly which passage of Scripture he and his wife Sandi had been studying before he called. *Because it would just figure that they had.* Anything less dumb-founding simply wouldn't have been possible that day. Not the way that God had gotten inside my head.

The crux of March 12 had come in the afternoon when I took a break from work and sat down to watch Todd Haynes' *Wonderstruck* on Amazon Prime. It's a quiet, mystical drama featuring Julianne Moore... and, as my sister Elane asked later that evening, what was I doing watching a Julianne Moore film? I hate Julianne Moore.

And the answer is, well, because that's the kind of day I was having. Where the world sort of stood itself on its end. I was already wondering what alternate dimension I had wandered into long before the Act III turning point of the plot of *Wonderstruck* arrived. I wrote of that plot in my review of the film:

> In the wake of an improbable "act of God," a young boy named Ben embarks on a quest to New York City to find the father he has never known. Haynes follows Ben on this trek while also telling us the more-or-less parallel tale of another child, a girl named Rose, who also sets out for the Big Apple in search of silent film star Lillian Mayhew.

Their stories inevitably intersect, as one might expect, given that this is a movie... right? No spoiler there. But Ben's and Rose's paths collide in a most unexpected and touching way.

And they intersect with these words: "I need you to be patient with this story. And I need you to read it slowly."

It was as if Todd Haynes and screenwriter Brian Selznick had spent the last two years of their lives conspiring to reach directly into my heart and pump it back to life. At 4:00 PM on March 12, 2018. As I sat on my couch in Des Moines, Washington.

I literally could almost not breathe, and shouted, "God, what are you doing?" As I summed up in my review,

> Art imitates life, lunkheads! If you look around you, really look around you, God—the Universe, the Earth Mother, Ahura Mazda, the Flying Spaghetti Monster, for crying out loud, if you so desire—is orchestrating things like you wouldn't believe.
>
> Like you wouldn't believe.
>
> Like. you. would. not. believe.
>
> To discover that, sometimes you have to be struck deaf. Some-times you have to learn to hear all over again. Sometimes you have to have things taken away that you thought you could not live without. Sometimes you have to let friends go in order to get them back.
>
> We all get thrown curve balls. And sometimes we get beaned... but that's not the only way to see stars. With a

little practice, who knows? Maybe you'll wind up wonderstruck.

So that's where these Wonderstruck notes come from. A different way of looking at life.

∎

Ole and Trufa

I recently needed to hire some landscaping help for my parents.

After a long search, I managed to track down Marcie and Loyle, eighty-seven-year-old twin sisters who do a lot of work for my various neighbors at Huntington Park. When I met them outside their Normandy Park home, they instantly remembered me—and asked how Jenn was doing.

Jenn had loved talking with the two of them when they had occasionally worked for our next-door neighbor Ouida, and had gotten to know a bit of their life story. They were greatly saddened to hear that Jenn had passed away.

In yesterday's mail, the invoice for my folks' yard work arrived from the Collins ladies. In a separate envelope, they had also included a card of condolence. Inside the envelope they had tucked three folded sheets of paper including the text of Isaac Singer's tale "Ole and Trufa."

I had never heard of this story about two leaves clinging in love to the baring branches of a tree at the onset of winter, but I set it aside to read later.

Last night as I went to bed, I grabbed a new book to start reading. I often have books sitting around waiting for "just the right time" to read. Last night felt like the right time to begin *The Mountain of My Fear*, mountaineer David Roberts' first book.

As I walked toward the bedroom in the dark, something fell out of the book. I stooped to look. It was several pressed cottonwood leaves that Jenn had collected at Wannacut Lake last July and tucked into the pages of *The Mountain of My Fear*. My brother-in-law Norman had given me the book that weekend.

I didn't think much of the significance of the leaves as I went to bed. This morning for my listening time, however, I picked up the story of Ole and Trufa, as translated by Joseph Singer in the pages of *The Atlantic* some decades ago and now long out of print.

If you haven't heard of it, it is a story of love and death, and of redemption, and this is it in a nutshell:

> Trufa awoke and to her amazement found that she was no longer hanging on the tree. The wind had blown her down while she was asleep.
>
> This was different from the way she used to feel when she awoke on the tree with the sunrise. All her fears and anxieties had now vanished.
>
> The awakening also brought with it an awareness she had never felt before. She knew now that she wasn't just a leaf that depended on every whim of the wind, but that she was part of the universe. Through some mysterious force, Trufa understood the miracle of her molecules, atoms, protons and electrons—the enormous energy she represented and the divine plan of which she was a part.

Today would have been Jenn's 46th birthday, which we celebrated prematurely last October with a "re-birth day." Awakening, indeed.

Jenn, like Trufa, now knows what comes next. How exciting!

■

Silence

Last night, I spent perhaps the quietest night I have ever experienced in the woods.

Most often I backpack in areas where there is running water. Even when I'm camped near lakes, there is usually the sound of brooks trickling into them or of tumbling water from their outflow.

The reason I usually backpack near running water is... well, I like water. And I don't like carrying water in with me. I like to be able to find it when I need it, not lug it in along with all the other necessary gear. A pint's a pound, as they say.

Lately, though, I've been experimenting with "dry camping" for the very reason that it forces different disciplines. It also opens the spectrum of where one can camp—and I've been wanting to camp in off-the-beaten-track places.

Or, in the case of last night, entirely off the track. Any track. Even game trails. (I did see one set of deer tracks and one small collection of elk droppings... but even those ruminants seemed to be, well, going rogue.)

I haven't been so off-trail in probably thirty years. The rain forest in which I camped was so isolated that there wasn't a sound of any kind, once the flickers went to bed.

Jenn had an extraordinary gift which she would, at times, interject into nature's silence. Music was in her very soul, and during her last couple of years she had the ability—witnessed only by me and her parents, I believe—to improvise musical settings for Psalms from the Bible. She would open a page from the scriptures, study it for perhaps two minutes, and then open her mouth to sing. Her melodies and the way that she would interpret the words of a particular Psalm were always enchanting and sometimes chilling. One particularly memorable instance at the end of a Waitts Lake pier in eastern Washington stands out.

But this is a gift I do not have. In fact, when I was basking in God's silence last night, the urge to sing did arise. Instead, however, a better instinct took hold. As I wrote,

> let us not speak of
> silences so sacred they
> are best unbroken

This is no indictment of Jenn, nor of her gifts. But it does clarify, for myself, how I am unique.

∎

Jane Stephenson

Jenn's co-workers at her final job, Regional Hospital in Riverton Heights, were so indescribably kind to her.

When she became critically ill soon after starting work there, for example, company policy allowed employees to give unused sick leave and vacation hours to other employees... and Jenn was the recipient of such generosity more than once. To the tune of dozens of hours of missed work time.

In addition to the wonderful and heartfelt sendoff Jenn received when we went on a New England cruise shortly before she was taken out of the workplace by narcolepsy, probably the act of kindness she most appreciated was the knotted-fleece blanket given to her as a get-well gift after one of her hospitalizations. A dozen or more co-workers, led by Jenn's colleague and friend Jane Stephenson, took a hand in tying the fringes on the cat-patterned fleece that was perfectly Jenn-sized.

I am in the process of packing up my house in preparation to sell, and just this morning I pulled the freshly laundered knotted fleece out of the dryer. As I was folding it, I thought, "I should get in touch with Jane and see if she would like to have this blanket!"

On my way home from lunch today, I saw a sign for a church rummage sale in Des Moines and decided to stop in. After browsing around a bit, I was on my way out and passed a woman standing near the door. After I was outside, it struck me... that looked like Jane Stephenson!

I walked back inside, and sure enough: it was. In the fifteen or so years I have known Jane, I have never just run into her... until today.

I went home to get the blanket, and Jane was thrilled to have it. "I guess this was meant to be," she said.

Yes, Jane.

And yes, Jenn. It was.

■

Christopher Hitchens

The late Christopher Hitchens and I by no means share the same worldview.

That does not mean I have had nothing to learn from the man.

In recent days, I have been trying to pin down the genesis of the mind-shift which has produced a year-long run of heightened awareness to and appreciation of serendipitous occurrences. The most I have been able to articulate to date is that my life would have been very different had Jenn passed away a year earlier; but something started changing in the early months of 2017 which allowed Jenn to accept and embrace her looming demise, and which also allowed me to start seeing God's hand directly guiding things. This has brought me great peace and joy, even through tragic loss.

This morning I followed the bread crumbs of my own story to answer that question: whence this mind-shift. It was buried in my own writing from May 4, 2017.

> Well, it's not hocus-pocus. And it's not the power of positive thinking. It's being responsive to what God is telling you and putting Him first. As we decode the recipe of our [own personal] journey from the clue-like ingredients God supplies, He "breaks through the stubbornness of our heads and hearts," to again quote [pastor Caleb] Mayberry. And we are then indeed "dealing with a whole 'nother animal."

I journaled those words in response to a sermon in which Caleb sought serious answers to the age-old human query, "Where are *my* 'signs and wonders'?"

But Caleb's words were not the catalyst; they just stirred the pot and crystallized some thoughts and spurred me to action. The real grist for my spiritual mill had come on February 28 when I read renowned atheist Hitchens' reflections on the Apostle Paul's "road to Damascus" experience.

This is what I wrote about that on May 4, 2017.

> "Great apparent coincidences," wrote the late Christopher Hitchens in his memoirs, "only occur to the intellect that has rehearsed and prepared for them."
>
> By this I took him to mean that miracles only appear to those facile enough to believe in them in the first place—though I'm not entirely sure, since Hitchens' mind and breadth-to-depth of experience were far greater than mine could ever hope to be.
>
> But I hazard a guess, nonetheless, that my human journey has been perhaps richer than his precisely because I began to "rehearse and prepare" for "great apparent coincidences."
>
> After all, the opposite is also perfectly probable: that one is likely to miss great miracles, if they do in fact occur, if one has rehearsed and prepared to *dismiss them* on the basis of *a priori* commitments.
>
> One doesn't change one's mind, Hitchens avers. "Your mind changes you." I agree with him on that point. But I also

believe that in 1993 my mind began to be renewed by God and that I have been in turn transformed by that renewal.

If we rely solely on ourselves or other deeply flawed human beings to shape our minds… well, good luck with that.

In March last year, thanks to Hitchens, I once again began to rehearse and prepare for great apparent coincidences… and to document them. To put myself out there and declare "This is what I believe, and this is what I see."

And the proof has been in the pudding, as they say. I have been living with, and embracing, great serendipity. I see God moving distinctly in the world around me nearly every day.

I don't expect that the world works this way for everybody, or that it should. And I don't expect that the remainder of my years will look like the most recent twelve months…

But you can sure bet that I will be rehearsing as if they might.

■

The Moment

Friday, March 9, 2018, Fidalgo Island.

That morning I was enjoying quiet time with God in a waterfront spa. As my friend Kaileah Akker says, morning is "the spirit's time. There are fewer rules at these hours. The veil is thinner—powerful hours to be invited into." So I was listening to that invitation, bathing in not only hot water and God's warmth but a beautiful sunrise. I was listening to Nathan Clark George on my MP3 player.

As I was doing my knee exercises, I heard a splash—and turned with horror to find my MP3 player had fallen into the spa.

DOA.

The rest of the day did not play out the way I expected, either. The spark of a warm friendship seemed to drown as well, and I returned to my marine retreat much earlier than I expected.

Later, having not much else to do, I of course disassembled the MP3 player and tried to dry it out, but it was no good. Throughout that long, solitary Friday evening, and worse yet, the very lonely Saturday morning that followed as my suspicions from the previous day were confirmed, it sat atop the fireplace in hopes that simple warmth would resurrect it.

But it was dead. I drove home to silence, the sweet soundtrack to my life gone.

■

Saturday, March 10, Des Moines, Washington.

Saturday evening I considered just throwing the MP3 player away. It wasn't good for anything anymore, not even spare parts or batteries.

Y'all sense a metaphor brewing here?

Late Sunday night, something told me: *You need to learn to be more patient; you should give this another try.* So I pressed the power button. Nothing. I pressed it again, harder and longer this time. Nothing.

Then I plugged in to external power.

In amazement I watched as the display came back on. And after it rebooted, I saw that the battery had not been dead after all. There was still life in the thing. It just needed a kickstart from outside.

Curiously, the "Now Playing" song was not what it was when the player went in the drink. In fact, it wasn't playing Nathan Clark George *at all*. Instead, somehow the MP3 player had chosen—out of a couple thousand tracks—to come to back to life playing Freddy and Francine's "The Moment."

> The moment that you find me
> You say that I've been blind to see
> You're the way to changing
> But I see you my dear

> Yeah, the moment that it's ending
> You finally stop pretending
> The time it took to build it up
> Just to knock it all down
>
> What we gonna do now
> Our love's on the line
> I can tell you I've tried
> But I lost what I found
>
> Run out of time
> We've run, run out of time
>
> Out of sight,
> We're out of our minds
> To make it right
> We've got to hope to find the time

Then came March 11, March 12… and *Wonderstruck*.

Plugged in to external power, indeed.

∎

Beauty

Can one become jaded to awe? I believe so, yes.

So much blessing pours into our lives on a daily basis, in fact, that we often walk right by glorious things with barely a reaction.

I shudder to think that I might have missed one such moment on the slopes above Fisher Lake while hunting with my father in the Alpine Lakes Wilderness on a perfect September morning in 1980. I was fifty or sixty yards above him on the slope as we moved slowly to the southwest, following the arc of the bowl above Fisher Lake through the bear grass, fir, and huckleberry. I had probably stopped for a drink of water from my canteen and looked down to see Dad pausing for his own moment of reflection. I grabbed my Pentax and zoomed to capture a stunning moment of a man in nature at its most gorgeous. The photo still hangs above my father's desk in his study.

I could have been so wrapped up in my own stuff, though, that I missed that moment.

I was reflecting on this tendency we have to turn the awesome into the mundane as I was completing the loop trail at Saltwater State Park this morning. A light mist was falling as I began my hour-long walk, but, by the time I ascended to the south rim of the park, full sunlight was falling through the trees and the air was beginning to warm.

I was so glad I had not let a little dampness scare me off at the outset.

Of all things, I began to think about Martin Sheen's performance in *Apocalypse Now!*, which tells the story of a U.S. Army captain sent upriver into the heart of darkness called the Viet Nam War. Along the way, he witnesses things that would astound and cow an ordinary soldier. Some of them, such as his encounters with Colonel Kilgore and Colonel Kurtz, still register with amazement on Captain Willard's face; but so many more, as when The Roach tells Willard he knows who's in charge at the Do Lung bridge, or Chief Phillips' death, barely warrant a reaction. Willard simply sees, and moves on. Sheen knows Willard can still be shocked; but he also knows how jaded the captain has grown to be.

The opening scene of the movie demonstrates how bottled up and closed off to emotion Willard has become, shut down to what Kurtz describes in his dying breath as "the horror."

But if you think about it, the same thing happens in our everyday lives with blessing! We are as saturated with goodness, when it really comes down to it, as Willard's stylized jaunt upriver is imbued with the macabre. The admonition to "stop and smell the roses" is not idle.

But the ways in which we incorporate and design comfort into our lives can deaden our sensitivity to beauty because it becomes so controlled... so expected.

By way of analogy, a wonderful home is like comfort food; a mature landscape design is like fine cuisine; yet pure, unadulterated nature is the best of nutrition for the soul.

I think I discovered that this morning because my home is for sale, and its "staging" feels too sterile. I was glad I decided to get out of my literal "comfort zone" and be wonderstruck, once again, by beauty.

■

Elissa Weisz

Elissa Leeann Weisz was asked to offer a high school graduation address in Anacortes yesterday morning. I was greatly privileged to be on hand.

In addition to other pearls of wisdom, Elissa closed her address by responding to well-wishing adults who have offered endless amounts of advice about how to protect herself as she ventures out into the great wide world. It's advice that has Elissa "kind of freaking out." But this is what she had to say about fear and the unknown.

> I don't have mountains of faith in my abilities to sustain my relationship with God. I know hard things are going to happen, and walking in purity is going to be a challenge.
>
> But I have mountains of faith in God's Story.
>
> I have faith that He paid the price for my sin. I have faith that He walked alongside me when the going was so deeply painful. I have faith that He carried me out of the Valley of the Shadow of Death—He didn't let me die in there. I have faith that although my dear friend died in that darkness, He is still good. I have faith that His ways and callings over my life are so much higher than my own.
>
> And, frankly, I have faith that, while I am away, you will pray for my relationship with the living Jesus.

Church, we are recklessly loved, yet terrified to fully receive that love. I think we know deep down that God knows and sees everything, and when we fully seek to receive His love in spite of our sin we have no choice but to live in submission—submission to His Story.

But He's teaching me that our fear of this submission is silly. It's silly because His Story for each of us is full of Him. And He is good.

It's crazy and confusing and I'm probably kind of failing the whole gig.

But I'm learning.

I am learning tiny little bits about my Creator, and it excites me, overwhelms me, amazes me, and calls me to big things.

Big, mysterious, unknown things.

I'm fifty-five, and I'm a little wonderstruck by this eighteen-year-old speaking the Spirit into my own life. What a blessing.

> You most demonstrate faith when you are able to confess, "I don't know what to do"… and move forward anyway.

■

Rusty Van Deusen

To be wonderstruck by this pastor is, in fact, to be wonderstruck by the Spirit of God.

This is because Rusty Van Deusen knows that the most important voice in the room is never his. You can feel that in his presence, and you can see it in his actions.

At a recent Sunday morning worship service at Christ the King Anacortes, Rusty had planned on preaching about the problem of fear in connecting with our neighbors; but the morning's plan jumped the rails a bit, particularly after a very stirring message from Elissa Leeann Weisz.

Rather than stick to the plan, Rusty easily recognized that the Spirit had other ideas that day… so instead of quickly seguing from Elissa's theme into his prepared sermon, Rusty chose to linger a while with Elissa's words. He then spoke briefly about how the Church can benefit from encouraging its youth—how instead of focusing on what they are not doing, it's more profitable "to see what God is doing in them and to point that out." Rusty sees great value in affirmation.

That Sunday, Rusty never got around to preaching from Numbers 13 or Joshua 2 or Isaiah 41. He only spoke for about three or four minutes on his planned topic. And that was perfectly okay with him. He felt that God had been very well served and worshiped on His own time and plan.

I spoke with Rusty after the service to offer my own words of affirmation, and he emphasized how important encouragement is, particularly to young people—how beautiful it can be "to dance with them a while, and then let them take the lead."

How beautiful are the feet of those who bring Good News… and let that News be God's, rather than their own.

∎

Chris Chesser

I had a long-overdue lunch with my old friend Harry Chris Chesser a couple of weeks ago.

As is usually the case when I connect with Chris, the universe held a few surprises for me.

Chris lives on the outskirts of Burien these days, so it was relatively easy for me to pick him up. On the way, I decided to run some errands. I maintain a post office box in Burien for my business concerns, and this was one of my stops that day.

I don't know if this happens at your own local post office, but sometimes when people get sent books they don't want they will just leave them out on a counter near the boxes.

As I breezed through the lobby, I noticed a volume sitting on a counter. After I walked by, I processed what had passed through the corner of my eye, and I thought, "Except for its coloring, that looks an awful lot like *Jesus Calling*."

That 365-day devotional was one of Jenn's favorites, and she had bought dozens to give to friends. I had never read it myself, but I was sure deeply familiar with it. "I bet it's the sequel," thought I.

When I returned from my box, I stopped to look. Sure enough, the book was Sarah Young's *Jesus Always*. I thought,

"I wonder if I'm supposed to pick this up for my friend Dawn." Like Jenn, she also is a fan of *Jesus Calling*. So, why not?

I grabbed it and headed out the door.

A couple steps from the car, I caught myself. "Why do I always think about other people, instead of myself? What if this book is intended for me? In fact, what if this book is intended for me today, right now?" I looked at it, and it had one of those built-in bookmarks—and had been manufactured with a particular page pre-bookmarked. I opened up the book to the randomly marked page and read.

> I understand you far, far better than you understand yourself. So come to Me with your problems and insecurities, seeking My counsel. In the Light of my loving Presence you can see yourself as you really are: radiantly lovely in My brilliant righteousness.

Just that morning, Dawn Thompson and I had been talking about the ways in which I have been learning to see myself as I really am, and the role that counseling (both formal and friendly) had been playing in that process of maturation.

Well. Huh.

I snapped a photo of that page on my phone. I got in the car, and as I held the book in my hand, another thought occurred to me. "Maybe this book is intended for Chris today. I know he's struggling a little right now, too." I put the book on the dash and drove over to Chris's apartment.

As I made the turn entering the drive to his building, *Jesus Always* slid off the dash onto the floor.

I picked it up and slid it into the door pocket, completely forgetting about it.

I had a great birthday celebration visit with Chris, catching up after not seeing him for nearly twenty years! He has fully recovered from his devastating bout with AIDS and has even tested free of HIV for fifteen years. But the long-term effects of the virus have been severe. He's been on disability for some time, has frequent seizures, and requires regular visits from his sister and a caregiver. His husband walked out on him a long time ago. He is often frustrated with his lack of mobility and with loneliness, though his online Google community brings him great joy.

After an excellent Thai lunch, we returned with leftovers to his apartment. As we pulled into a parking spot, Chris spied *Jesus Always* poking up out of the door pocket.

"Is that a devotional?" he presciently asked. All he could see was the top of the pages—not even the spine.

Why, yes, it is. A 365-day devotional.

"Can I have it?"

But of course! How serendipitous.

Later that afternoon, I texted the photo of that one page to Dawn.

She immediately replied, "Is that from *Jesus Calling*?"

Well.

I guess I really was meant to pick up that book.

And it really was meant for Dawn. And for Chris. And for me.

∎

Chesterton

I caught up with my old friend Stephanie Cortes last night over coffee, and at one point she asked me, "What do you tell people when they ask you about the point of suffering?"

It was not an idle question, since Stephanie knows quite a bit about what my late wife endured and what I went through at her side for fifteen years—and about the suffering in her own life.

In reply, I did not bother to mention the empathy that I feel for those who are suffering; because there are moments when you feel like there is no point, when you either want to (or do) let go of the things that tether you to hope or to reality or to the future. That's where the rubber hits the road, as it were. But what I did reply was, "In the middle of it all, what we lack is perspective." And that's perfectly true.

I told Stephanie that there are two foundational concepts that can help see one through suffering.

The first is what G.K. Chesterton called the willingness to find "gold in the gutter." In *The Defendant*, Chesterton wrote that the pitted kitchen knife we discard would have been a miracle to a Neanderthal. So, he says, "the things we call 'bad' are things which are simply not good enough for us."

We must always keep this in mind. If we are honest about our own experiences, we will admit that we (and those we know) have weathered many "bad" things that eventually brought about very desirable results. In the moment, though, "bad" was definitely bad.

Second, like it or not, we are always preparing ourselves for how we will handle tragedy—for better or for worse. It's a principle that Laurence Gonzales describes at length in *Deep Survival*. It's a principle that I saw played out in my late wife's final months.

Just as "love is a long series of choices, all in the same direction," the way that we deal with suffering is the product of long years of training. How you think about it in this very moment, years before you encounter it, is already shaping how you will deal with it down the road.

Months before she died, for instance, Jenn decided how she would pass. And she passed lovingly, generously, and without complaint, even though she suffered greatly. And the grace with which she passed was a great blessing to many.

Bryan Stevenson is an attorney who is the author of a wonderful book entitled *Just Mercy: A Story of Justice and Redemption*. One story in particular dominates the narrative thread of the book, but Stevenson recounts a variety of other remarkable incidents of redemption along the way.

I have been wonderstruck by many of these. Last night I finished *Just Mercy* and was blown away by the story of a woman whom Stevenson encountered outside a New Orleans courthouse. He assumed that she was a relative of one of the unjustly imprisoned men whose freedom he had just secured. "No, no, no," she replied. "I just come here to help people. This is a place full of pain."

She told Stevenson how she had first come to the courthouse, to attend the trial of the boys who had murdered her sixteen-year-old son—how she had cried and cried for weeks during the trials, and how she cried even harder when the accused were found guilty and sentenced to life in prison, because the sentencing did not make her feel any better. How a stranger simply held her for two hours while she cried, unable to leave the courtroom after the verdicts were read.

"Well, you never fully recover," she told Stevenson. "But you carry on, you carry on. I didn't know what to do with myself after those trials, so about a year later I started coming down here. I don't really know why. I guess I just felt like I could maybe be someone, you know, that somebody hurting could lean on."

That is redemption. That is a choice which gives meaning to suffering. That is beauty.

That is finding gold in the gutter, as Chesterton wrote:

> Now it has appeared to me unfair that humanity should be engaged perpetually in calling all those things bad which have been good enough to make other things better, in everlastingly kicking down the ladder by which it has climbed. It has appeared to me that progress should be something else besides a continual parricide; therefore I have investigated the dust-heaps of humanity, and found a treasure in all of them. I have found that humanity is not incidentally engaged, but eternally and systematically engaged, in throwing gold into the gutter and diamonds into the sea.

I have found that every man is disposed to call the green leaf of the tree a little less green than it is, and the snow of Christmas a little less white than it is; therefore I have imagined that the main business of a man, however humble, is defence.

I have conceived that a defendant is chiefly required when worldlings despise the world—that a counsel for the defence would not have been out of place in that terrible day when the sun was darkened over Calvary and Man was rejected of men.

The universe knows a thing or two about suffering; and it does not want us to despair. It wants us to choose hope, to believe beyond hope in a purpose and plan greater than ourselves and our limited powers of perception. To love first, and ask questions later.

Most probably we are in Eden still. It is only our eyes that have changed.

∎

The Defendant

Many years have passed since I last read G.K. Chesterton's *The Defendant*, which became a seminal part of my spiritual reawakening 20 years ago. Many phrases from his introduction have stuck with me, however—and I quoted heavily from it in my Wonderstruck note yesterday.

The weight of its truth really settled heavily upon me yesterday when I re-read the full "Introduction" after posting my note. And I was overwhelmed by what Chesterton wrote over one hundred years ago.

"The pessimist is commonly spoken of as the man in revolt," Chesterton observed. To amplify, cynics and critics are hip, styled as the voices crying in the wilderness, speaking truth to power, railing against the staid status quo, and so on. The rebel is, in popular thought, a revolutionary.

"He is not," Chesterton counters. "Firstly, because it requires some cheerfulness to continue in revolt, and secondly, because pessimism appeals to the weaker side of everybody, and the pessimist, therefore, drives as roaring a trade as the publican."

The more things change, the more they stay the same, it seems. Conditions in 2002 were not so different than in 1902, when Chesterton penned his intro. I certainly know that I, for one, found it hip (and funny) to live as a pessimist in my younger years. I even proudly (and glibly) passed myself off as an "optimistic pessimist," explaining that's "it's best to expect the worst so that a good deal of the time you are pleasantly surprised."

That was code for: "I'm afraid of getting hurt by expecting too much of myself, or of others, or of God. So I will protect myself by expecting very little."

The problem with that position is that we do, in fact, create our own reality to a great degree. I know for certain that I missed out on many good things in the first decades of my life simply because I didn't expect to find them.

Not until my thirties did I discover what Chesterton knew: "The person who is really in revolt is the optimist, who generally lives and dies in a desperate and suicidal effort *to persuade all the other people how good they are*" (emphasis mine).

Again to amplify: To be an optimist is to be the one who is *really* swimming against the tide. Pessimism is easy; it rolls downhill and gathers very little moss. Optimism: It's hard… extremely hard, if you know anything at all about how the world works.

Chesterton continues:

> It has been proved a hundred times over that if you really wish to enrage people and make them angry, even unto death, the right way to do it is to tell them that they are all the sons of God.
>
> Jesus Christ was crucified, it may be remembered, not because of anything he said about God, but on a charge of

saying that a man could in three days pull down and rebuild the Temple.

Every one of the great revolutionists, from Isaiah to Shelley, have been optimists. They have been indignant, not about the badness of existence, but about the slowness of men in realizing its goodness.

The prophet who is stoned is not a brawler or a marplot. He is simply a rejected lover. He suffers from an unrequited attachment to things in general."

And, I'd add, to hurting people in particular.

Optimism is not practical. Optimism is not pragmatic. It hopes for things beyond its obvious reach and expects the best where the world says, "You'd better be careful!" Being optimistic invites pain. But we always have choices; and which is preferable: the pain that may result from expecting the best or the pain that is inevitable if we do not? You are going to change the world, one way or the other.

I conclude with an extended quote from the lyrics of Switchfoot's "The World You Want":

> You start to look like what you believe
> You float through time like a stream
> If the waters of time are made up by you and I
> If you change the world for you, you change it for me
>
> What you say is your religion
> How you say it's your religion
> Who you love is your religion
> How you love is your religion

All your science, your religion
All your hatred, your religion
All your wars are your religion
Every breath is your religion

Is this the world you want?
Is this the world you want? You're making it
Every day you're alive
Is this the world you want?

Serendipity

> "How can one grow fully into the potential of the gift that is our life?"

I shouldn't have been on the North Cascades Highway.

It wasn't my idea to be there at all, as good an idea as it was. No, I had originally planned to be on the Tonga Ridge trail for the weekend. But a wonderful friend had suggested doing the Winthrop Rhythm and Blues Festival, and I readily agreed to change my plans. After all, music is good; a road trip is better; the Methow is grand; and time with excellent friends is priceless.

I shouldn't have been driving alone that day, either. Remember that part about good times with friends? Well… another change of plans. Good thing I value flexibility! But I still love music, road trips, and the Methow. And I had tickets in hand for the festival, plus a pre-paid reservation for a tent spot at Big Twin Lake. All I had to do was… load up and go. So I went! Why not?

> "Even when there are other pressing tasks, when there are heartbreaks and children to attend, even then, especially then, a good life responds to beauty."

Since I was making the trip alone, I ended up with a little extra driving time. To make sure I didn't get too sleepy, I decided to break up the drive a little. About three hours in, I stopped at the North Cascades National Park Visitor Center. Restrooms were on my mind. So were chips and a soda, perhaps. I had packed a light lunch, expecting to augment it a little along the way. So I poked my nose into the tiny gift shop.

I really shouldn't have been in there. I knew there'd be no vending machines in a National Park gift shop. It'd be t-shirts and trinkets. But what the hey! It's vacation, right? What I had not thought about was books.

Well, to be perfectly correct I had thought of books—but had thought of stopping at a bookstore in Winthrop, since I had recently finished the last unread book not in deep storage while I'm trying to sell my home.

> "It starts as a small feeling in the core, a story remembered, a way back to mystery."

I really don't like buying brand-new books. I'd rather adopt them. But here I was contemplating becoming father to a brand new bunch of ideas, courtesy of someone else's womb-like brain… and typesetting.

I found a very intriguing title on the shelf: *NATURE LOVE MEDICINE: Essays on Wildness and Wellness*. The cover of the book is a photo of the red rock formations outside Torrey, Utah, one of my favorite places.

So I picked up a book I shouldn't have. I have been enjoying it immensely, devouring it while I'm not doing the things I should be doing while at a music festival.

To be fair, I arrived a full day early so I could miss traffic, poke around Big Twin Lake, drive into Twisp to check out a silversmith's shop, and drive up into the Methow hills. I made time for the unexpected.

Have I mentioned I like driving?

> "With implausible frequency, I find just the thing I need exactly when I need it."

One of the places I discovered is Sun Mountain Lodge, at the end of a lovely 20-minute spin past Patterson Lake—itself a fine enough destination. The Lodge, however, is a swanky resort perched atop a high bluff overlooking the site of the festival. It's posh—but with a public restaurant and bar, and informal enough that non-guests don't get accosted by stiff staffers looking down their noses at the hoi polloi.

I had a good gander around the place and decided I would have to return for lunch or dinner while I was in the area. Then I went to the festival.

I apparently *really* wasn't supposed to be there. Not a good fit for me at all. Say no more.

After ditching the festival just a couple hours into the opening night's program, on the way "home" I passed an old ruined homestead on the site of a U-pick berry farm. The type where literally you pick, you pack, you pay. Nobody on site at all. Honor system.

The ideal Golden Hour light was already gone, so I decided I'd come back the next night, half an hour earlier, and snap some pictures. And pick some raspberries.

I went back to Big Twin to read some more about the healing power of natural experience.

> "The nature of my work bids me pay special attention to happy accidents."

The next day I did a whole bunch of things I shouldn't have done when I'm supposed to be at a festival. The best was spending four hours exploring Falls Creek, fifteen or so miles up the Chewuch River road. Then I stopped in for another stab at the festival. I didn't even last an hour. 'Nuf said.

I was getting into a funk. But Plan B was about to kick in, big time.

> "Serendipity is the guiding twinkle of my creative process."

After arranging to meet another friend for breakfast the next day in Twisp, I had settled on dinner in the bar at Sun Mountain Lodge. An experienced hand at dining alone, I knew to take along a book to read, as Sun Mountain would probably not be the place for a hand of Solitaire. I took along *NATURE LOVE MEDICINE*, of course.

The next chapter, I saw, was an essay about serendipity. The quotes you see scattered throughout this note are from that essay.

> "Close attention to specifics allows the practitioner to both see what is there, and conceive what is not."

On the drive up, the county road ends just past Patterson Lake at the Chickadee trailhead, just at Thompson Road. I had felt my heart surge as I rounded that corner the day before, and I felt the same burgeoning in my heart again.

Something really good was about to happen.

On the final approach to the lodge, I saw that two carts full of guests were out for a horse-drawn experience of the Methow highlands in the evening light. Hard to believe that a place like that offered reasonably priced meals.

I helped myself to parking and a walk through the expansive lodge lobby, replete with a fully-taxidermized bison and other various game animals. The bar hostess seated me in a north-facing alcove of the dining room containing exactly one table for two. She described it as "the best seat in the house." She was not wrong.

I shouldn't have been there, of course. I was an interloper from Big Twin Lake campground, not some high roller from Medina or one of the defense lawyers attending the weekend conference.

Across an aisle from me was a low divan with a coffee table. I would be dining quite alone, apparently.

After ordering, I dove into the essay "Serendipity, Sculpture, and Story" by Edie Dillon.

I was dumbstruck to be reading things I had been waiting all my life to hear someone else say, ideas that had been percolating in my brain for years via bits and pieces of science, philosophy, and theology osmosed but never chewed on or consumed explicitly.

At one point, I literally put the book down and almost said out loud, "Why am I reading this *now*? Why at fifty-five years old am I having this clarity of thought about how the world works and my place in it?"

In part, because I shouldn't have been there.

Serendipity.

> "The naturalist and the artist both endeavor toward senses sharpened to the magic things…"

I pondered the question for a few moments and my meal arrived. The server also brought a drink for a young man who had sat down on the divan across from me. I had been tempted to talk with him a bit earlier, but I couldn't tell if he simply preferred to be alone with his thoughts. We had not made eye contact.

I was just about to resume my reading when I thought, "Well, maybe one reason I need to be reading about serendipity right now is that this is not simply a chance encounter." One of countless that we perhaps dismiss as random every day.

I ventured a standard male-to-male query, "Business or pleasure?"

> "…a feeling that the divine encompasses and is manifested in each detail of the material world."

And so I met Eric Peterson last night at Sun Mountain Lodge. He is a thirty-three-year-old man celebrating his fifth anniversary. He lives on Highway 97 three-and-a-half miles up Swauk Pass canyon and runs the Blewett Brewery in Leavenworth. We talked at length about the same country we have traveled and treasure in the area—Old Blewett Pass, the County Line trail, the Teanaway hills, the Cooper River trailhead. The oddities of Leavenworth. Our mutual aversion to techiness in everyday life. Our affinity for nature. Both of our first experiences with the Methow. The history of fire in the region. The amazing power of life to regenerate itself and redeem what seems like irreversible devastation and tragedy.

> "What is required of us is a willingness to cultivate serendipity."

Eric was having a little down time and a drink while his wife enjoyed the pool. I think we were both grateful for the brief encounter of kindred spirits in that rarified atmosphere.

Not to overstay my welcome, I said my goodbyes after paying my bill and went out to the verandah to finish Howe's essay.

> "This day was graced with serendipity, an ordinary thing gone magic, a new and different ending to a very sorry tale. We know that young men die and mountains burn. We know that life is full of sorrow and change, and we sometimes hope that change brings new beauty."

Just... wow. This day certainly was graced with serendipity, in fact and in word.

Shouldn't this be my year of grief? Shouldn't I be morose and despondent, almost suicidal at times? Shouldn't I be mourning the loss of the greatest gift I'd ever been given?

Well, no, I *shouldn't*. Because Jenn and I learned gradually about serendipity without even knowing it—about looking for the unexpected and reading the divine into it, about being continually wonderstruck by the gifts we receive even though we logically, even morally, feel like we shouldn't have received them. Though of course the word "wonderstruck" hadn't come to me until March 12 this year, through another amazing multi-day chain of serendipity—another tale of life beginning where there should only be ashes.

> "Awareness of serendipity is not dumb luck; it is a developable quality of mind that arises from openness to the unexpected."

Jenn and I came together through unbelievable circumstances to live a flawed but nonetheless fairy tale romance. It could have ended tragically, but it did not. It ended beautifully, if far too soon.

And then it became time for a new ending to my story.

That story is still in process... and I am being patient with it, reading it slowly.

It's more a beginning than an ending. Because the universe wants to amaze me. I am convinced of it. I can see no other way to live.

> "Is there anything in the natural world that does not express with exquisite and terrible and intricately fitted loveliness?"

■

I did make it back to the raspberry patch at twilight after stopping to enjoy some eye-to-eye contact with a doe in a newly-mown alfalfa field. I shot a few photos, and found, to my surprise and delight, that someone had just picked an entire flat of ripe berries, ready for the packing. I paid for a pound and left a note of thanks. I felt like I was thanking the entire universe that evening.

Returning to the campground, I shared the bounty of berries with a young family tenting next to me. The toddler had called me "Papa," and I took his enthusiasm as a kindness that I wished to repay in some simple way. Who knows what may grow from the seeds of those berries?

> "The gift of serendipity is that we can use it to create a new story, or, in our current predicament, a new ending to the same story."

My day ended with a text from the most excellent friend who "should" have been on the trip with me.

It read, "Hi, Greg! Winding down here for the day. Can you talk tomorrow morning? Say, 8:00?"

Oh, yes. I have so much to tell.

■

Butterfly

I was reading *NATURE LOVE MEDICINE* at sunny Big Twin Lake on Saturday morning and paused to reflect on how well I have been loved in recent years.

As I did so, a yellow swallowtail fluttered by and brushed my chest. Jenn had always said that if she visited me after she died, it would be as a butterfly. I said aloud, "Hello! Are you going to come land on me?"

After paying a visit to our Yaris and alighting oh-so-briefly on the Scotland plate affixed to the front bumper, the butterfly did indeed return to me and settled onto my left thigh. It sat with me for about five minutes.

Aside from visits that Jenn and I made to the Butterfly House at Pacific Science Center, I had never had a butterfly land on me until that morning. I took it as an affirmation that, yes, I have been loved—and loved very, very well, loved for who I am and who God made me. And that God indeed has wanted me to know all along how much He loves me.

And I am content with that knowledge, whatever comes next.

When the swallowtail flew away, I asked aloud, "Are you going to come back?"

After fifteen or twenty seconds, it did return and again alit on my thigh, for a couple of moments.

Gratitude overwhelmed me.

■

Backcountry

I did some pretty nutty things in my younger days, but backpacking cross-country from Fisher Lake to Marmot and Jade lakes the summer of 1983 was one of the nuttier. Repeating that same trek in 1993 at the age of thirty-one was another!

I was reminded of the relative insanity of those hikes this week not only because I was on the trail to Fisher Lake for the first time in decades, but because the unimaginable happened.

At the Tonga Ridge trailhead, I ran into a pair of backpackers who had just returned from *that very trek*, following exactly the same off-trail route we had used in '83 and '93.

These dudes were thirty-eight years old. Crazy.

Nobody, and I mean *nobody*, hikes into Marmot Lake via Fisher and Ptarmigans. The route involves the five-mile, 1600-foot elevation gain route into Fisher, a 1.5-mile route-finding scramble into Lower Ptarmigan, and then an off-trail bushwhack of another mile into Upper Ptarmigan. This is where we camped for the first night during our treks.

From the Ptarmigans, it's 1200-foot elevation gain in a half-mile scramble up a trail-less brush-covered slope to the north shoulder of Terrace Mountain, followed by a mile or so of open rock slide traverse across the east face of Terrace. Once you come to the end of the south Terrace ridge, there's a game trail that drops 800 feet abruptly to Marmot Lake via a fresh rock slide scramble… and then another abrupt 600-foot gain at the beginning of a two-mile jaunt to Jade.

Whew! Open country the whole way, baking in the sun between 5000 and 6200 feet elevation. In 1983, our second night camp was at No Name Lake between Fisher and Jade, and it snowed. In 1993, we were toast at Marmot. Both years, we finished our journeys on the Snoqualmie Pass side of things.

Only young people or people who *feel* really young—or people who *think* they feel really young—attempt such things. In 1993, we thought we felt young, or at least we *wanted* to feel young.

The hikers we met on Tuesday certainly looked fresh at the end of their trail. It was kind of loony checking off the mileposts of their trip with them, comparing notes about journeys made a quarter century apart.

While I was reflecting on this relative insanity this morning, I exchanged messages with my young friend Max Losee, with whom I rafted the Grand Canyon in April. He commiserated with me about the bugs in the Cascades this week, mentioning that he'd run into them during a run through the Enchantments on Saturday.

A run. Through the Enchantments.

Kids these days.

■

Peter Alford

Peter Alford first attended Harambee Church early last summer.

Jenn being the extremely extroverted person she was by that point, and Peter being the relative extrovert that he is, not many Sundays had passed before the three of us were thick as thieves, as they say. Before long, Peter had visited our home a couple of times, even spending one Sunday afternoon watching a Seahawks game with us.

As Jenn's health declined, I started leaning more and more on Peter as a friend and peer. Young as he is, he is a fount of wisdom and probing questions which never fail to make me think more deeply about my walk with God.

On more than one occasion over the last several months, Peter has been the catalyst for some very profound spiritual insights. He was with me on the afternoon of March 11, in fact, asking, "What does it mean to love yourself?" in the midst of a spectacular string of serendipitous events that stretched over several days. That four-day weekend pretty much turned my world upside down, in an awfully good if painful way. (March 12 was when I discovered *Wonderstruck*, as you may recall.)

But Peter is not only a fine source of wisdom. He is also a dandy wit.

Last night our weekly talk found us at Redondo, and the evening concluded with a walk along the seawall. At one point as we were talking about the temptation to superiority or pride, I made a rather pithy observation: "If you really *are* the better man, the best you can do in any context is to simply *be* the better man."

And I followed that up by saying, "I need to write that down!"

To which Peter replied: "Wonderstruck by Self."

I was glad I had a slice of orange in my mouth rather than a swig of Diet Coke.

■

Disposable Cameras

Today was a very good day for closure of a sort.

On April 4 this year, Max Losee and I set out for the Grand Canyon. The trip was a time for me to be reborn: to reconnect with wilderness in a spectacular way; to test my rehabilitated left knee, and find out if it—if I, with it—had a future; to be wonderstruck, and be inspired to write about the feeling.

I was so unbelievably blessed and enriched by the trip. Max and I naturally took a lot of photos, many of which have already been shared with fellow rafters and with Facebook friends. Max's disposable camera, however, has had an interesting journey since we returned to civilization, such as it is, on April 11.

First, it's difficult to find a place to get those suckers processed. Max managed the trick after several weeks, however, taking his to the Shoreline Fred Meyer. He bided his time picking up his prints and scans, though, not seeing that there was any particular rush.

He returned after several weeks to find... the photo finishing department *completely gone*.

The store was processing so little film that it no longer made sense to use floor space and staff hours for the service, so everything went... including Max's unclaimed photos!

The manager was adamant; there was nothing he could do. "But," Max protested, "those were photos of the Grand Canyon!" Max could tell that the manager's chagrin was profound, so he left his contact info with him. Surely, Max reasoned, digital copies of the scans must still exist somewhere.

The manager did not hold out hope; but a couple of weeks later, Max got a call from Fred Meyer: The photos had indeed been located on the scanning computer which had been repossessed to "central storage" from the Shoreline location. Max was told he could come pick them up...

...only to find that the photos had again been lost in transit.

I arrived at Max's place this morning for a couple days and nights of working meetings. The last time I stayed in the guest house here at Richmond Beach, I had been tempted to write about how wonderstruck I was by "The Love Shack" and its setting; other more pressing topics, however, supplanted the thought—and the feeling. I also figured I'd be back at The Love Shack and could write about it then.

Today was apparently that day, in quite an unexpected way. Smoke from the Twisp fires hovered in the offshore flow all day. Who'd have thought, during my previous visit to Richmond Beach, that I would soon be moving to Twisp?

One of the first things Max mentioned when I arrived was that he had just received another call from Fred Meyer, reporting that his photos had been found yet again! We left to pick them up immediately, so that they would not become lost once more.

The negatives yielded some wonderful shots, of the canyon, of the water, of Nankoweep—of Max and I, and of me snapping a photo of Max at the Little Colorado.

It was so good and so timely for me to revisit the Grand Canyon today.

And God bless the things that serve their purpose well. Cameras may not last forever, but this one, at least, kept giving and giving for several months. And the memories will last a lifetime.

■

Heaven Knows

One of the things I needed to find a home for last week was Jenn's sheet music.

As I was musing what to do with it while out taking a walk, I ran into Brenda Blair, who had at one time come close to subbing on piano for Jenn with the Huntington Park Chorus. I delivered a box of music to her later in the week.

I just got an email from Brenda thanking me for the gifting. "I found a couple of books, especially holiday music, that work for me nicely," she wrote, "and it was fun to go through all of these pieces. Jenn must have really been accomplished; some of these are really difficult for me!"

Yes, Jenn was quite accomplished at the keys, and very much attached to and inspired by them. I distinctly remember the day I realized, "I get to marry a pianist!" A lifelong dream fulfilled.

While I was going through Jenn's sheet music last week, I came across a song she wrote—one that I did not know about.

> Last night as I sat by her bedside
> My daughter said her bedtime prayer;
> Then with a waning sense of childhood innocence
> She asked, "Mommy, why is the world unfair?

Why do people grow old?
Why does everyone have to die?"
I panicked at first—how should I answer her?
And then came this reply:

Heaven knows why the world's unkind,
And Heaven knows the questions that fill your mind,
And so it goes:
Only Heaven knows what Heaven knows.

I waited for her to accuse me
Of avoiding her inquiry.
But her questions went on with the innocence gone
From a child who sees how the world can be.
"Why do children go hungry?
Why do nations go to war?
Why do we fight just to prove we are right
And then forget what we're fighting for?"
I answered,

Heaven knows why there's so much pain,
And Heaven knows why peace is so hard to attain.
And that just shows
Only Heaven knows what Heaven knows.

"But there's so many things that I don't understand.
Why must babies fall down before learning to stand?
Must branches be pruned for trees to grow strong?
What makes one lie right and another wrong?
Will I ever know what Heaven knows?"
The silence told me she'd asked all her questions
At least for now—but one thing worried me.
Did she accept my reply, or merely wonder

If I had answered superficially?
I hoped that she'd never stop wondering
Why there's pain and death and war.
As I kissed her good night and reached for the light
She said, "Mommy, just one more.
If Heaven can answer my questions
When I get there, do you suppose
That they'll answer them all?"
Then I turned down the hall
And whispered,

Heaven knows.
Heaven knows the answers you'll find
As you try to make peace with your troubled mind.
But still it goes
That only Heaven knows what Heaven knows.
Baby, only Heaven knows what Heaven knows.

Yeah. Wonderstruck.

■

Prunella vulgaris

I was introduced last evening to the identity of this plant... not in the field (though I had often seen it and wondered what it was) but through a book.

In the essay "Heal-All," Robin Wall Kimmerer remarks that "the scientific name of the genus Prunella sounds like the name of a wicked fairy-tale step-mother."

I had a good hoot at that, suspecting that what Kimmerer was summoning to mind was not a fairy tale, but *Fawlty Towers*... whose eponymous landlords were played by John Cleese and... wait for it... Prunella Scales. Vulgar, in a way, to be sure... but no fairy tale. Nope. Anyhoo...

Kimmerer's essay was not about the finer points of English satire. No. It was about *Prunella vulgaris* itself, and the healing properties for which it has long been known.

At the essay's opening, the scientist in Kimmerer is conducting an experiment: placing *P. vulgaris* poultices on one thorn-scratched arm while placing placebos on the other. Within an hour of lounging in sun-drenched grass, the treated scratches have all but vanished.

P. vulgaris is known by many names: Heal-All, Wound-wort, Heart of the Earth, Carpenter's Weed, "the one we put on spider bites," or its German root "Brunella," which refers to its extract's ability to treat sore throats. The point for

Kimmerer is that we have lost much of our sense of the natural healing properties of the world—and the essay calls us to recapture not just the facts of healing but a way of talking about nature that recaptures lost wisdom.

She invokes native language from her own heritage which refers with respect to all living things as "beings," rather than with the sterility of generic pronouns.

I certainly couldn't quibble with the author about the lost wisdom aspect. In all my years of wilderness experience, even the decade I spent hanging around with Master Gardeners, not once do I remember anyone talking about *Prunella vulgaris*—much less trying to make a field poultice from it. In fact, in my experience with landscape maintenance I have been regularly told to regard it as a weed and eradicate it. Which I always found strange, because a healthy bed of *P. vulgaris* is awfully attractive.

But the real kicker came when Kimmerer wrote the following:

> We live in a pharmacy of healing beings. Certainly plants like Heal-All, but medicine also lies in the song of a Hermit Thrush, the scent of firs and the shadows of clouds running like a herd of sheep across the mountains. It is the encounter which is healing. It is generative of curiosity, of wonder and awe that makes us feel deeply human and at home in the world. Psychologists have documented that the sensation of awe has health-promoting properties

The publisher left out the period which concludes that paragraph, and I find that poetically appropriate. I am wonderstruck, even.

Naturally, I had zero trouble locating some Heal-All during my walk this morning.

Take that as you like.

> It is the encounter which is healing. It is generative of curiosity, of wonder and awe that makes us feel deeply human and at home in the world.

■

Brewminatti

This falls into the "just too strange for words" category.

I spent Saturday at the Brewminatti Block Party in Prosser, Washington. Prior to attending the Block Party, I knew nothing about Brewminatti. It's a wonderful little coffee shop and music venue that's housed in the "Historic Mercer" building on 6th Street. Friday and Saturday nights, I stayed in a guest suite at the Historic Mercer, directly upstairs from Brewminatti.

Saturday evening was the one and only time I have ever set foot in Brewminatti. I had a wonderful piece of pie.

Tuesday evening I was watching the *Follow This* episode "Black Survivalists" on Netflix. The segment is reported by Buzzfeed's Bim Adewunmi. At the 2:35 mark, Bim sits down at her laptop to communicate with a survivalist trainer…

…and what to my wondering eyes should appear, in that five-second clip of Bim at her laptop, but the Brewminatti logo reversed on the window behind her.

Wow. Seriously?

I thought, "Oh! Brewminatti must be a chain. It must be famous. And Bim is obviously at one of the other stores."

But no. There is just the one Brewminatti.

And it is *not* famous. At least, not outside Horse Heaven Hills, as far as I can tell.

So, yep. Buzzfeed's Bim Adewunmi at Brewminatti in Prosser.

Reminds me of a line from *Serenity*: "How weird is that?"

■

Finding Home

Jenn and I came to Huntington Park West Homes Association in a most unexpected fashion: My first view of our home was actually through my rear-view mirror!

On a February Friday afternoon in 2010, we had just finished setting up Jenn's first photo gallery exhibit in Kent. It was an enormous leap of faith.

In the wake of Jenn's disability, she had been emotionally (and physically) lost for two years, devastated at loss of an identity which she had clawed out of the ashes of suicidal depression and eating disorders. At the end of 2008 she defiantly declared a new identity… as a photographer. Over the next year, I also developed a new identity as Jenn's curator and promoter, a role I would continue to play until her death almost a decade later.

That initial exhibit was an enormous commitment, an investment of thousands of dollars in large-format prints and frames. We both knew that if she failed at this new venture it would almost literally kill her.

During the drive from the gallery to our next appointment, nervous energy filled the Jeep. I turned to Jenn and asked, "How does it feel to be entirely in God's hands?"

We were early arriving for a rehearsal of the Huntington Park Chorus, which Jenn had recently started accompanying on piano. (My folks had already lived in HP for several years, and Dad directed the Chorus.)

Having some time to kill, we decided to drive through the Park and see what was for sale… thinking that maybe Jenn's folks could find something they liked. For some time, they had been wanting to move from the Federal Way home that Bob Cram had built, and the housing market bust of 2008 had brought prices at the somewhat exclusive Huntington Park down somewhat.

The very last For Sale sign I spied, in my rear-view mirror, was tucked away at the end of the 10th Avenue *cul de sac*, the middle unit of a triplex. "Hang on a sec," I said to Jenn. I backed the Jeep down the block and parked.

The asking price was ridiculously low, so we peered through the windows. While the Chorus rehearsed, I made some phone calls and found out that the home was bank-owned and that we would likely qualify for a first-time homeowner's loan. By Monday afternoon we were pre-approved, and within a week our offer was accepted. Six weeks later we were out of our Burien apartment and into our re-roofed, re-floored, and re-painted home. Paying less in mortgage than we had been paying in rent!

And we hadn't even been looking for a house to buy. Unbelievable. I guessed that's what it might feel like to be in God's hands!

Early April was our move-in. 2010 ended up being such a good year, and many more wonderful years followed. Huntington Park was such a tremendous place for Jenn. And for us, and me.

And how did that photo exhibit go, the one which put us at Huntington Park with time to kill prior to that chorus rehearsal? It was killer, with more than $2000 in photos sold during its run. It gave Jenn a sense of purpose to go along with our new home.

■

Exactly one year ago as I write this, Jenn made the decision to go on hospice care. So fitting that earlier today I put that home once more in my rear-view mirror and left Huntington Park to begin a new life in Twisp. I have just turned fifty-six, and even though HP is a 55-and-over community (with a 20% exemption!) it's clear that it's time for me to be somewhere else.

And my path to Twisp has been as serendipitous as Jenn and my discovery of our Huntington Park home. As serendipitous as the story of our marriage, in fact. It is simply time for the next adventure.

Farewell to the greenbelt, to the pea patches, to the Saltwater State Park trails, to the birdbath and all its delightful visitors, to easy visits with Jenn's parents (who did, in fact, find a home across the street!) and my folks and The Shy Pilot, to all our delightful friends at HP, to so many wonderful memories of Jenn and of Us.

Thank you, Huntington Park, for incubating me, for seeing me come alive again, and for letting me leave the nest!

■

The Walls

The most recent wedding ceremony which I officiated was five years ago today aboard the *Skansonia*. My good friends Jeff Walls and Elisabeth Leitch became husband and wife that day, culminating a most improbable romance.

I introduced Jeff and Elisabeth, not at all thinking that they would start dating, much less marry—contrary to the insistence of my own late wife, who was convinced that I was playing matchmaker. No, I just knew both of them quite well and simply thought they'd have a lot to talk about.

I've known Jeff since about 1988, when he and his sister were just kids. His dad Randy and I worked together at Quinton Instrument Company, and I procured Seahawk season tickets for Randy and his wife, Virginia. From time to time, Randy would bring Jeff to a game, and I especially enjoyed gametime chats with Jeff when he began working at the Renton Cinemas and we would have movies to talk about in addition to football.

When Jenn and I started thinking about launching the movie review website *Past the Popcorn*, I recruited Jeff as one of our featured reviewers. He had already published more than a thousand movie reviews for his own site by that point. Elisabeth started writing for *HollywoodJesus.com* in 2004, during the height of the site's popularity. By 2006, she was working as my assistant editor, managing a staff of reviewers in the

Bay Area. Even though our weekly meetings were conducted by phone and email, I did get the chance to meet her in person a couple of times at press events and the Annual Gatherings of HJ's staff.

When Elisabeth decided to relocate to the Seattle area in 2011, I suggested to the two of them that she meet Jeff for a press screening… and the rest, as they say, is history—sweet history.

Serendipity, my friends, serendipity.

■

Privilege

Yesterday morning I read an essay by Alberto Búrquez entitled, "Plants, Health, and People of the Forbidden Mountains."

The essay culminates with an account of a visit that the Sonoran research ecologist made to the remote village of Guajaray deep in the Mexican Sierra Madre. The essay's conclusion is evocative enough, but the rather static, scholarly, and clinical prose that Búrquez offered left me cold.

His ideas, however, did not. Rather, they percolated in my brain throughout the day. As I was driving down the Methow Valley to Chelan last evening, enjoying the golden hour light, I started thinking about my choice of Facebook timeline banner, a photo I shot earlier in the week of a lone tree on the west ridge above my new hometown of Twisp. I realized that, without thinking about it very explicitly, I had chosen a rather metaphorical image.

Then I wondered: Do people think I'm running away from something, plunking myself out here in the middle of nowhere all by myself?

This isn't true at all, of course. I'm right in town, surrounded by people, and I've already met and made several new friends here, in addition to the people I already knew. So I'm not transforming into a hermit. Quite the opposite, really.

But as I drove and reflected on my lunchtime conversation with new friend Terry L. Pisel, I conceded that part of the appeal of the move is that, yes, for at least the next year I am going to be experiencing an endless stream of new things by which to be wonderstruck: a couple dozen new restaurants, cafes, and bars to try (none of them Asian, alas!), countless new galleries and shops to explore, hillside after mountain after canyon to hike, skis to buy, snow to shovel, mud to avoid, flooding rivers and fires… not to mention night after night, dawn after dawn, day after day full of landscapes and starscapes and skyscapes to ponder and photograph.

If you've known me long at all, though, you know that I've always been an adventurous soul, even right where I lived in Des Moines.

And that thought brought me back to Búrquez and his essay. "People longing to leave their homeland," he wrote, "are unhappy persons, said Czech novelist Milan Kundera," referencing Kundera's novel *The Unbearable Lightness of Being*, famously made into the film starring Daniel Day Lewis. "Many people live oblivious of the marvels surrounding them," Búrquez notes; "some others long to leave."

I confess that during the "middle years" of Jenn's fifteen-year illness my appetite for life and adventure was, um, somewhat blunted, shall we say. I really wanted nothing more than for it all to be over with. But I did not rediscover being wonderstruck by life only *after* Jenn's passing. No, the great privilege of life itself began creeping back into me several years ago, in spite of—and perhaps *because* of—the very real need to confront the meaning of suffering.

"If we go through life in the express lane, never taking the roads through the small towns of suffering," writes poet Subhaga Crystal Bacon, "we have no experience, no understanding of it. We haven't seen its byways, tasted its flavors, smelled its odors. It's not possible to live without suffering, so to pretend to do so by avoiding or ignoring it, is to pass through life being only partly alive."

And so, one morning three or four years ago, I lay in bed with Jenn, the brilliant January light streaming through our eastern-exposure windows, and started contemplating all the great blessings that the "needs" of her illness brought into our lives. The greatest of all of them was slowing down, checking out of the "normal" rhythms of American life. And at the time, the best word I could apply to all of that was, "Privilege."

Privilege, in the face of, and due to, suffering.

"Perhaps the unhappiness leading to escape," continues Búrquez, "is a consequence of utter ignorance on the role of natural resources in our lives." His prose is indeed a little cold, no? But his point is sound. No matter where we are, no matter what our circumstances, we have at least two options: a desire to escape unhappiness; or a conscious choice to open our eyes, look around, and be wonderstruck at what we find.

And here is a lesson on that score from the terribly mundane. I was doing some product testing the other day which involved textual proofing of a series of interview questions in parallel with video playback of the recorded questions. Because of technical considerations, the screen on which the text appeared was upside down.

I don't believe I have ever done proofreading upside down before.

Interestingly, I noted nearly a dozen typographical errors in that sequence of seventy-plus questions, including three or four punctuation errors… in spite of the fact that this was my fourth pass through the text.

So one doesn't necessarily need to escape one's world in order to see it in a new light. All one needs to do is stay right where one is—and turn the world upside down.

Or turn oneself upside down.

Turns out I'm pretty wonderstruck by Búrquez after all.

■

Foreign Agents

Traveling internationally never fails to remind me of the time that John and I smuggled counterfeit currency to Mexico.

In 1985, airport security was, in a word, lax. Those old enough to recall the world of travel prior to 9/11/01 will recall that every unticketed Tom, Dick, and Harry in the world could walk right up to a departure or arrival gate. There were no TSA checkpoints, and when circumstances were right—say, on a Southwest Airlines Christmas Eve flight, for a first-hand example—you could board without even showing ID. If you had a ticket, you were generally good to go, and it didn't much matter where you got the ticket or whose name was on it. All that really counted was that the seat was paid for.

I was working at Boeing in early 1985, and my security clearance was being processed because the initial tests of the Peacekeeper Launch Protection System were coming up at Vandenburg Air Force Base. This young greenhorn had been tapped to lead the on-site team with Air Force brass.

Life was good. I was a gainfully employed bachelor with a bright future. Naturally, I was spending money like it was going out of style.

My housemate John Adami and I decided we needed some fun in Mazatlan, so we booked an off-peak week in the late-winter sun. I was already an old hand at Señor Frog's and the

Golden Zone hotspots and was determined to show John, ahem, what a good time looked like, as it were.

When we got to SeaTac airport, the terminal was nearly deserted, and our Mexicana Airlines flight to Mazatlan was sparsely populated. Of an entire DC-10, I think perhaps fifteen seats had been booked. The trip was shaping up nicely.

With our early arrival and the lack of ticketed passengers to process, the mood at the departure gate was unusually relaxed. Our guard was down. While John and I killed time and joked around with ease, a sweet little old Norwegian lady from Ballard tottered up to us and asked us if we could help.

We were young and jovial and obviously interested in having a good time—so I imagine that translated, in her mind, into "helpful."

Or "naive." Hopelessly naive.

She explained that her son Aarvid had recently married and was honeymooning in Mazatlan. The trouble? The bride and groom were having such a good time that they had run out of cash.

Could we possibly be kind enough to take some traveler's checks down to Aarvid?

I inquired of old Mrs. Aarhus (at least, that's what her name sounded like) where Aarvid was staying. "El Cid? Oh, sure! I know where that is. We're staying at Los Sabalos, and that's right in the Golden Zone, too. Dropping off some checks at El Cid would be no problem!"

Mrs. A was charmingly pleased and produced a sealed, unmarked white envelope nearly half an inch thick. John and I blithely took the parcel, which I tucked in the inside breast pocket of the slick leather jacket I had purchased in Mazatlan during my previous visit. She showed us a Polaroid of Aarvid so we'd be able to identify him south of the border.

About fifteen minutes into the flight, as the pre-flight distractions and associated endorphins faded away, my brain finally settled into, um, thinking.

And I got to thinking about traveler's checks.

I thought about picking up my own traveler's checks for the trip, and how—as those old enough may also recall—you had to *sign the checks* once when you bought them at the bank.... and *countersign them again* when you cashed them.

Airline security may have been lax, but they had money issues locked down in those days. The person who cashed a traveler's check most definitely had to be the same person as the one who bought it.

Ergo, what I had tucked in my jacket pocket was equally most definitely *not* a packet of traveler's checks.

Crafty little Mrs. Aarhus—or whoever that devil really was—had really duped the two of us. I started running through various scenarios in my head—steaming open the envelope in the bathroom, admitting to a flight attendant that John and I were idiots, and so on—and all of them ended up in just about the same place: a Mexican jail. There's no way a Mexican pilot on a Mexican airliner was going to just turn around and deposit two dumbass gringos back in Seattle.

But there was one plan that perhaps did not involve a Mexican hoosegow: delivering the package as instructed. This was also the easiest plan to pursue because I wouldn't have to discuss a thing with John, to whom nothing untoward had occurred.

And still I wondered—as we started our descent, literally and figuratively—what was in that packet. Contraband? Drugs? Smuggled documents? Maybe a stack of $1000 bills, which were still in circulation at that time?

As we stepped off the plane, I sure hoped that packet wasn't drugs… or anything else that *smelled* suspicious, because the whole scenario had just gotten a thousand times worse: This was off-peak travel, and John and I were in an airport that was not only near-deserted, like SeaTac had been, but was also disproportionately populated by Mexican soldiers with automatic weapons… and attendant German shepherds.

This was not the co-ed-friendly Spring Break Mazatlan I had come to know and crave. This was like a Mexican version of the Turkey I'd seen in *Midnight Express*. Anybody old enough to remember *that*?

Oh. My. Gosh.

I thought I was going to have a heart attack as customs officials took their sweet time processing the two of us under the watchful eye of green-clad sentries and their tongue-lolling pets. I have never been so close to sheer panic.

And then, having just cleared passport control without any near-death incidents, who should immediately swoop upon us but Aarvid Aarhus… or whoever he *really* was?

So much for the rendezvous at El Cid.

This was starting to feel like a really scary episode of *Moonlighting*, but without the humor, and without Cybill Shepherd. Bummer.

Without so much as a thank you, Aarvid grabbed the proffered package and left with a small entourage of largish men. During our shuttle ride to Los Sabalos, a cab with Aarvid et al screamed by. I pointed them out and took the opportunity to share my worst suspicions and fears with John—who was naturally aghast.

We were relieved, at least, that we were shed of the packet and of Aarvid.

We settled into our room and went straight out to the beach to enjoy a relaxing drink under the thatched umbrellas. Like the airports and the hotel lobby, the beach was vacant. It was late afternoon, and John and I were literally the only ones on this particular stretch of Golden Zone beach.

Except for the occasional soldier who would saunter by, carbine at the ready. For what, I was not quite sure.

Oh.

There was one other guy on the beach, too—another gringo marching purposefully down the beach from the north… up where El Cid was.

And this man on a mission took an abrupt ninety-degree turn just below us and came directly to our shelter and knelt between us.

He wore a blue Hawaiian shirt with several open buttons, and heavy gold chains gleamed against the sunburn on his curled chest. A Panama hat perched atop his head. He introduced himself as Dennis and spoke with a thick French-Canadian accent.

John and I kept our eyes shielded behind our dark glasses and mumbled the tersest negative replies to his queries. Did we need anything? Booze? Pills? Girls? Cuz he knew a guy who could get us whatever we wanted. Whatever. Really. He swore. Dennis could be sure we had a good time while we were in town and just wanted to see that we were properly taken care of.

We assured Dennis we were perfectly okay on our own, thankful that he finally tired of our relative silence and wandered off whence he'd come.

And, I guess, we *were* perfectly okay on our own. Other than the fact that just about everywhere we went that week, Dennis would show up about five or ten minutes after we would—always alone, never occupied with anything other than, um, looking silently out for our welfare.

After a couple days of this, we pondered trying to take some action to stop it all. Were Aarvid and Dennis in cahoots? Were they trying to lure us into their trafficking so we could take another package back to Seattle?

Were maybe Dennis and Aarvid on opposite sides of the law, with Dennis trying to find out what we knew about Aarvid?

Should we go up to El Cid and confront Aarvid? Should we confront Dennis?

Should we contact police? Oh, that Mexican jail issue again!

For better or worse, we decided to just ride out the week and make the best of it. At the very least, the vacation turned out to be memorable.

Upon my return to work the next Monday, I received my security clearance briefing packet. The top sheet was titled, "10 ways to know that you have been contacted by a foreign agent."

As I read through the ten bullet points, I was not surprised in the least. They were all very familiar to me and very fresh in my memory. I had seen *every one* of them at least once during the previous seven days.

Toward the end of the year, the story broke that a counterfeit currency ring had been operating in Vancouver, B.C. and funneling the funny paper through Seattle. I honestly have no idea if Aarvid or Dennis or sweet Mrs. Aarhus had anything to do with it, or whether John and I had in fact been unwitting parties to the scheme, but it sure seems the most likely explanation.

Years later, though, when it became possible to Google such things, I did find a photo of Ballard fisherman Aarvid Aarhus bringing in a sailfish somewhere in warm Pacific waters. At the very least, I had not imagined the name.

Though I have to say, Aarvid is still kicking around the Seattle area… so I've used "Aarvid Aarhus" as a pseudonym here, rather than his real Norwegian name.

Just in case he and his darling mom really *were* involved in counterfeiting.

You can't be too safe with such things, even after thirty-some years.

My security clearance told me so.

∎

Fairies

They say money doesn't grow on trees. But it certainly appears to do so on the mysterious coin-studded trunks dotted around the UK's woodland, reports the *Daily Mail*.

Just outside Rosemarkie on Scotland's Black Isle peninsula, a wooded path follows Rosemarkie Burn to what is known as Fairy Glen. About a mile upstream from the car park are a pair of waterfalls to which locals and other visitors, like me, have been streaming for hundreds of years.

The falls themselves are not remarkable to anyone who has lived around actual mountains. While the scenery in much of Scotland is impressive indeed, it's no accident that the Gaels in this area had dozens of words for hill: *beinn*, *sgùrr*, *stac*, *meall*, *sìdh*, *cnoc*, or *dùn*, to name but a few. But none of them equates to "mountain." Hence, the waterfalls that flow from these hillocks bear not much resemblance to those found in places with peaks whose height quintuples those found in the Scottish highlands.

I still like waterfalls, though, even small ones. So I eagerly hiked to Fairy Glen at the end of my day. But what really jazzed me about this place was not the falls but the "money trees."

The first one I spied lies in the pool at the foot of the upper falls. It caught my eye immediately because it looked from a distance as though it had been riddled by woodpeckers. I thought it would make a nice foreground for a shot of the upper falls.

When I got close I realized that the log's odd texture was due to hundreds, if not thousands, of coins hammered into it over long decades. I soon discovered that other logs around the pool had been similarly graced.

Locals to whom I spoke explained that the custom originated to appease the local fairies—in much the same way that we throw coins into a wishing well… or leave teeth under our pillows, since teeth are apparently a superior currency to those feisty imps.

And it turns out that "this is a thing" across the UK. And belief in the power of fairies must be pretty profound, because none—and I do mean none—of these thousands of coins have been prised out. After all, as one fellow visitor put it, if one must already appease fairies with cold, hard cash, what might an actual disgruntled fairy do once it had been robbed?

Fascinating.

Personally, I was thinking what a wonderful Thai dinner I might have with only a few minutes of moderate trouble.

But I bet fairies would be really peeved about Thai food purchased with purloined pounds.

■

Forgiveness

Twenty years ago today, Jenn's heart changed. Miraculously so. I was there to witness the event.

I was visiting with Jenn at her daylight-basement apartment on Sand Point Way. We were leaving for a road trip to Utah in two days and were going through details concerning the trip.

My well-intentioned human plan was to propose marriage to Jenn while we were in Utah. But I was not at all confident that my plan was going to be fulfilled. An inner conviction had been telling me that something drastic was going to change in Jenn's life before I could propose; I didn't know what that was going to be, but I knew that it hadn't happened yet.

While we sat by the window, Jenn began telling me again about the pervasive anger in her life. Depressed since twelve years old and a committed cutter by sixteen, Jenn found herself in a sexually and emotionally abusive relationship upon graduating from high school. She had the courage to walk away from that... and, mixed up with deeper depression, Borderline Personality Disorder (BPD), eating disorders (ED), and suicide attempts, right into a series of affairs with married men.

After several years, treatment for depression and ED were pretty effective. But the anger behind her relational history was not so easily addressed. For nearly a year, we had both been slowly walking each other through our sexual histories—and there was no mistaking the bitterness attached to Jenn's. The sex had all been consensual—but most of the married men with whom Jenn had been involved were much older and had abused their positions of authority, being Jenn's pastors, counselors, professors. And they had all *known* about Jenn's history before becoming involved with her. She was, as sexual predators would well know, an easy mark.

And one characteristic of BPD is a predilection for engaging in sexual relationships with men easily identifiable as despicable... and hence disposable. Choosing cads for lovers is an effective way to make one feel better about the self one loathes. "He must be a loser if he loves *me*." Oddly, these men were all genuinely in love with Jenn at some level. The sheer challenge, perhaps?

As we talked in the fading golden hour light, Jenn's anger heated up more than usual—and it became directed at me. "Why aren't you upset?" she demanded. "You should be angry with them on my behalf!"

I explained that what I felt was more akin to pity than anger. As near as I could tell, each of these men was as broken as Jenn had been at the time, if not more so, and were themselves more in need of mercy and compassion and healing than further blame or retribution. They clearly had done wrong—but not maliciously so. They were misguided and selfish in their actions; but they were not evil men.

Jenn herself had been the recipient of the kind of compassion that Jesus had shown the woman caught in adultery (by cronies of her equally adulterous lover) and dragged before him for stoning; and I pointed out that Jesus showed mercy not because she was a woman, but because she was presumably remorseful and deserved mercy.

Like that woman, and like Jenn herself, these men had not gone on to serial affairs. They, too, had changed their ways.

Jenn had a hard time taking this all in and became even more angry with me. At the same time, she could see that I was deadly serious—even sorry to have to say such hurtful words to her. She could see that my heart was breaking with love.

And then her own heart broke. In a visible wave, years of bitterness and resentment washed out of Jenn like a soiled flood. She instantly broke down sobbing—not from further anger, but from joyful release.

Afterward she said it was as if the Spirit of God had invaded her soul and forcibly pushed darkness out of every corner. I believe that Jenn needed to fully forgive herself before God could work that miracle in her life, before she could honestly extend forgiveness to the men who had wronged her. I felt honored and awestruck to have been a party to and witness of that process. In the years that followed, Jenn made contact with each of those men and was reconciled with each of them. They contributed notes of tribute that I published at Jenn's celebration service, and I count them as friends today.

The universe does want to surprise us. It wants to remind us that the things which hurt us are also the very sources of hope and healing—that great beauty follows in the wake of great calamity.

The pain of Jenn's life cannot be underestimated or downplayed; but if you knew Jenn at all, especially in her last years, you saw the love and joy in her eyes and felt the love flow from her heart. All of that was not *in spite of* the pain; all of that flowed *from* the pain, from wounds that were healed—and from a heart that invited a spirit of healing.

Twenty years ago today, I witnessed a miracle; and it was the sign—the one I had been waiting for—that I would be her husband.

∎

Wind

Twenty years ago tonight, Jenn and I pitched our tent in an aspen grove a couple thousand feet above the Capitol Reef canyon floor in Utah.

We had driven the Jeep as far as we could up a long-abandoned road, and then carried all our gear further up through yellowing aspen. As we ascended, we stopped to watch a bull elk come crashing through the grove, his head tossed backward so that his antlers wouldn't get snared in the thick, low-hanging branches.

We managed to get camp set up and start grilling our steaks just before dark. Later, as we settled in for the night, winds started to pick up… and before long turned into a full-force gale.

At 7000 feet, we were isolated and exposed.

Chances of a tree falling and crushing our tent were pretty good. This late in the season, with snows right around the corner, if something happened to us, nobody would find us until the following spring.

As far as Jenn could tell, however, I was perfectly calm. And as long as I was calm, she was calm.

I went outside to lash our tent to an already-downed twenty-foot tree that lay alongside. Soon our alternately billowing and collapsing tent was dragging the tree down the hillside. Jenn and I lay beside each other wordlessly. I was actually quite terrified and didn't think we'd survive the night.

And then the strangest thought went through my mind. *If Jenn says anything to me, she'd better call me "Wilbur," cuz if she calls me "Greg" I'm gonna lose it.*

Now, Jenn knew that the nickname I acquired in college was Wilbur—and that there were many mutual friends and even nephews and nieces who called me that. But Jenn had never used that name for me.

Why on Earth did I want her to start now?

During that long, scary night I had plenty of time to answer that question. And I did not like the answer I came up with. I wanted Jenn to call me Wilbur in that moment of crisis because it was more than a nickname; it was even more than an identity I had acquired. It was, in fact, an alternate persona I had been developing for myself since I was fourteen or fifteen years old and finally found a name for while I lived in the dorms at the University of Washington.

Wilbur was popular. He made things happen and knew things he couldn't possibly know. He knew how to make doors open, literally and figuratively, and things generally went his way. He was confident and took control of a room when he entered. People noticed him and responded favorably. He mastered life in the outdoors and could survive with a pocketknife and a coat. He was bold and adventurous.

Greg was unpopular. He lacked confidence, and did things wrong all the time. He was a geek and a nerd and was awkward and lacked physical grace. When he entered a room nobody cared, unless they wanted to tease him. He expected to be bullied and cowed easily. He never wanted attention, and most often preferred to be alone. He didn't have a clue what to do in the outdoors.

So that night, that very particular night, my survival instincts told me that I needed to be Wilbur and not Greg.

Fortunately, I guess, Jenn never used my name at all that night. So I was free to masquerade as Wilbur one last time. But by morning, I knew for sure that if I were to propose marriage to Jenn, I was going to need this fractured-personality thing fixed.

I went into therapy not long after Jenn and I returned from Utah. My therapist helped me learn that my bifurcation was a survival mechanism that helped me deal with years of bullying and a deep-seated (and incorrect) perception that God wanted to punish me for being weak and evil.

As scary as that night was, it was probably one of the best things that ever happened to me—and to Jenn and me as a couple. Wilbur needed to get pushed to his breaking point, and God did it through the wind that night on the flanks of Thousand Lakes Mountain.

■

Flaws

Twenty years ago today, I proposed to Jenn at The Lodge at Red River Ranch outside Torrey, Utah. She, of course, accepted.

On October 10, 1998, we had beat a hasty retreat from our campsite high up on Thousand Lakes Mountain, where I had intended to propose, and wound up in town a day early. So the proposal did not go as I had planned; but the way things worked out was infinitely better than I could have asked or imagined.

I knew that Jenn had issues with engagement rings, so I had forgone the usual route for proposal. Instead, I decided to give Jenn an uncut diamond when I proposed and suggest that we wait to have it cut and set in a ring until some later time—perhaps our 25th anniversary.

When I produced the diamond in Torrey, I told Jenn its story.

I was living in Bothell during those years and found a small designer of custom jewelry at a crossroads south of Woodinville. I inquired as to whether the jeweler might be able to procure an uncut diamond, and he said, yes, of course. He could contact one of his suppliers in New York.

When I came in to pick up the diamond, he told me he had found me something very unique: a twin tetrahedron. Instead of the typical pyramidal crystal you might be used to seeing, this diamond was two crystals, fused at their base. Reportedly a rare occurrence in nature. This meant that when we had the stone cut, we could have matching diamonds set in matching rings. Beautiful!

Jenn was thrilled with the story behind the diamond—and after we talked about it, we decided we would go ahead and have the diamond cut upon our return from Utah.

A few days after taking the diamond back to the jeweler and selecting wedding bands, I received a call from the jeweler. And it was bad news. It turned out that the twin tetrahedrons shared a common flaw at their fused bases—and that if the diamonds were to be separated, the process would ruin both gems.

Because of this common flaw, the diamonds were in fact inseparable! How poetic.

We decided to leave the gem uncut and have it mounted in a pendant instead, also incorporating a red heart-shaped gem which Jenn's sister Patty had given her into a custom setting that we left to the jeweler to design.

When we went to pick up the necklace, we were early for the appointment and browsed through the jeweler's small shop. Jenn spied an especially beautiful piece in a lighted display case in the center of the room. She gasped and said, "That's gorgeous! I hope my necklace is as beautiful as that one!"

The jeweler walked up behind Jenn and said, "That *is* your necklace!"

What a wonderful surprise.

Jenn and I indeed had our faults; but we were so perfect for each other.

■

Affirmation

We weren't even supposed to be in Torrey, Utah, on Sunday morning, October 11, 1998.

We were supposed to still be up on Thousand Lakes Mountain, popping out of our tent into a grove of snow-trunked aspens, all in golden-leaved splendor against a backdrop of cobalt sky and red-rocked spires. But a windstorm had knocked us out of the hills a day early, so we loaded the Jeep and headed into town.

And now here we were rolling out of luxurious beds at The Lodge at Red River Ranch. It being Sunday, and us being newly engaged, we thought it a good thing to find a church to attend and ask God's blessing. This was especially important to me, because I had serious doubts about whether Jenn and I should marry. I had been ordained to the ministry in 1997 and had thought at the time that God intended me to remain single. Throughout those spring and summer months of 1998, as Jenn and I explored the idea of what romance might mean for us, I was consistently dogged by doubts.

Was this all just an illusion? Was it "The Last Temptation of Greg," some bizarre supernatural plot to either test my resolve—or distract me from my real purpose?

Were Jenn and I just supposed to be good friends, but neither lovers nor husband and wife?

So, even though both of us had prayerfully and soberly discerned that God intended us to be together not just in ministry but in marriage, and even though we were now officially engaged, I simply could not quell the noisy chorus of dissent in my heart and head. I craved affirmation that we were doing the right thing.

Off to church we went.

There was one option in Torrey: Rainbow Christian Church, a tiny one-room cabin just off the highway in the center of town. When we arrived, about six or eight regular attenders were already there, almost all of them elderly folks in their sixties or seventies. We introduced ourselves to the pastor, Boone Johnston, who said, "Call me Boonie." He was an affable, outgoing bear of a man, who looked (and spoke) an awful lot like an older John Larroquette.

Boonie was also inquisitive and soon learned that I was also a pastor, that Jenn and I were both active in leadership at our home church, and that Jenn was a pianist. Within a few minutes, Boonie returned to us with a couple of requests. First, might I be willing to pray the benediction at the close of the service? And, since the church's regular pianist was ill, could Jenn accompany the hymns that morning?

And so we found ourselves helping conduct the service that day at Rainbow Christian Church, two out of the roughly ten people in attendance.

After the hymns, Boonie got up to preach. He brought his Bible and notes to the podium and arranged them neatly. He then paused, looked up, and said, "It is my habit to prepare detailed notes for my sermons. But I also believe that when the Spirit speaks, we need to listen. Today, I am setting aside my prepared sermon and will instead speak on Ephesians 3."

And he proceeded to read from Scripture, concluding with these words:

> Now to Him who is able to do immeasurably more than all we ask or imagine, according to the power of the Spirit that is at work within us, to Him be the glory in the Church and in Christ Jesus throughout all generations for ever and ever! Amen.

Jenn and I were in shock.

This passage of Scripture had first come to my special attention the very first time I visited Jenn's apartment near Northgate. In her bedroom, there was a large whiteboard with this passage, Ephesians 3:20-21, written in Jenn's beautiful, bold hand. Above it she had written, "My Prayer for Greg."

And she had been praying those words for me before we had even dated. We had adopted that as "our Scripture," recognizing its unique value for us—because I could not imagine God wanting to bless me, while Jenn had the hardest time asking God for what she needed because she didn't believe God cared.

The idea that the universe wanted more for us than we could possibly conceive was something very new to us twenty years ago. And here we were, attending church together for the first time as an engaged couple, a thousand miles from home, serving God together in the company of strangers, with

Boonie listening to the Spirit telling him, "Preach from Ephesians 3."

Even without the powerful affirmation of purpose that we felt that morning, we never got over the feeling that our rendezvous with Boonie was one of those "divine appointments" that people sometimes whisper about.

The feeling deepened the following summer when we decided to move our wedding date up from July 1, 2000, to August 22, 1999. We wanted Boonie to participate in the wedding service... but my attempts to contact him were not only unsuccessful, they were mysteriously so. It was as if Boonie had never even existed!

Less than a year had passed, but the church was no longer called Rainbow Christian Church. It was now Torrey Baptist Church... and the woman who answered the phone said that there had never been a Boone Johnston at Rainbow.

Nobody I contacted in town, including the proprietors at Red River and the wranglers at Hondoo Rivers and Trails, knew anything at all about Boone Johnston. He wasn't listed in the online white pages. Boonie had simply vanished without a trace.

I did finally locate Mr. Johnston a few years ago, however; but that's a story for another day.

All I know is that Jenn and I felt the hand of God that Sunday morning twenty years ago today, telling us, *Yes. This is the blessing I have for you. Have confidence in it, and go and be fruitful.*

■

Change

In an essay entitled "Environmental Generational Amnesia," the University of Washington's Peter H. Kahn, Jr., talks about the ways in which we, individually and as a culture, gradually become adjusted to progressively degraded "new normals" in our environment.

It's a classic example of the figurative frog who slowly boils to death in a heating pot of water because, while he could have jumped out at just about any time, he doesn't since the temperature change is so gradual that he doesn't notice it. So he boils to death.

When it comes to the environmental degradation that Kahn talks about, he uses his research with children in Houston as a classic example. Even though the city was, at the time, classed in the top ten most-polluted cities in America, inner-city Houston children who knew what pollution was still did not consider Houston polluted—because it was normal to them.

We generally fall too easily into the trap of accepting progressively less ideal conditions as normal. And then we regularly ask, by way of self-justification or excuse, "But what am I supposed to do about it?"

One good first step, as Kahn advocates, is to start thinking consciously about this pattern of degradation—to acknowledge it, to walk around recognizing that nothing stays the same: that everything is always in the process of changing, even the oceans and the mountains, the moon and the sun, the Kuiper Belt, the moons of Saturn. Your mom. Your worst enemy. Your best friend. Your own bad self.

Knowing that change is inevitable, then, do we just cede to generational degradation and accept that we will leave our kids—hell, leave ourselves tomorrow or even later this afternoon—a worse-for-wear world?

Or do we take that second step, with every bit of non-crisis-management energy we can spare, of devoting ourselves to leaving things better than we found them?

Of bringing peace and joy to our online conversations instead of bitterness, fear, and rancor?

Of choosing words of encouragement with our kids instead of barbs or criticism or misplaced hazing sarcasm?

Of extending the same benefit of the doubt to the accuser as well as the accused?

Of choosing to believe the best, rather than the worst, about the next person you meet?

Change is the best friend and ally you will ever have. Embrace it. It's about time to jump out of the pot, wouldn't you say?

■

Revolutionary Love

"We are tired and raw," wrote Valarie Kaur in an email Friday, "and we have reason to feel hopeless."

I know a lot of people who feel like that. I have felt that way many times and lived in that emotional space for several years not all that long ago.

It's no sin to feel hopeless, and I would never, ever say to someone, "Well, just buck up. It could be worse."

Of course it could. It *always* could. But to anybody who's in crisis, the current crisis is the worst—the one at hand that must be lived, must be survived.

What consistently strikes me about Kaur is her message of hope in the midst of despair.

I first ran across her in a New Year's Eve address from a couple years ago that went viral not long after. It was easy to see why: because Kaur rightly divines that the solution to all our societal ills is an irrational devotion to the transcendent power of radical love. She draws her own inspiration from a spiritually driven faith and the power she has derived from being a mother.

Kaur, a Yale-trained lawyer and Sikh activist, is passionate about America and its future. "The founders of the nation," she continued in her Friday email, "invoked words whose power even they could not comprehend—freedom, equality, justice, and the guarantee of life, liberty and the pursuit of happiness.

"These words seized the imagination of the peoples for whom they were never meant," she wrote, rightfully pointing out that this inspiring vision has bled over into generation after generation, with an increasingly franchised populace rising up "to labor for these words and bleed for these words. They dreamt of an America that has never been, yet still must be—a nation for all of us."

Are you hopeless? she asks. "It is okay to feel hopeless in any given moment. Hope is a feeling that waxes and wanes. What matters is whether we choose to show up tomorrow—and labor anyway."

Are you angry? she wants to know. We can "honor our rage," she says, while at the same time knowing that "revenge and resistance will not sustain us in the labor." Why? Because resistance will "burn us out, or worse, turn us into what we are resisting."

The way to channel energy, she says, is to focus not on resistance but on rebirth. "Resistance points us to what we are fighting *against*, rebirth to what we are fighting *for*. Resistance narrows our focus to removing bad actors from power, rebirth expands our focus to remaking those institutions of power. Resistance marshals the energies of revenge, rebirth the energies of love.

"This is why I believe that Revolutionary Love is the call of our times: the choice to enter into labor for others, for ourselves, and for our opponents."

It's a beautiful vision for the future, for all people, and one that consistently moves me. "Today we breathe. Tomorrow we push."

Revolutionary love. Oh, yeah. I know someone else who talked about that a lot, a couple thousand years ago…

"Every breath," sings Switchfoot's Jon Foreman, "is a second chance."

For God's sake, let it start today. Breathe.

And then *push*.

Joffrey Hooks

Yesterday morning I heard the most striking message about the meaning of suffering.

"God uses controversy to engage us cognitively," pastor-educator-poet Joffrey Hooks said. Meaning, simply, that sometimes God needs to get our attention.

Preaching from 1 Peter 2, Hooks specifically pointed out that the purpose of suffering is most often not some grandstanding opportunity for gaudy miracles but the patient shaping of our spiritual maturity. A pretty basic spiritual point, but it sure felt to me like a slap upside the head.

Duh.

Given his familiarity with the subject, the Apostle Peter noted in that letter that Jesus provided us with a pretty decent model of the response to suffering. "When they hurled their insults at him, he did not retaliate; when he suffered, he made no threats. Instead, he entrusted himself to [the God] who judges justly."

Boy, is that an example we sorely need in America today.

Hooks acknowledged that most of us have come to the point of wondering, "When will all this suffering come to an end?" I certainly know that I have. But Hooks also rightly observed that when we are driven to ask, "God, what are you doing?"

the answer is most often, in one way or another, "Setting you free."

The end goal of the spiritual life is not ease and comfort; it is maturity and freedom. It is the ability to entrust ourselves to the power of the universe rather than the very limited power that we ourselves possess. It is coming to the point where we can honestly declare, says Hooks, "I am free."

> I am free from shame, I am free from guilt, I am free from the power of this pain and the power of this suffering. I am free from the weight of it because I have the weight and the power and splendor of God upon me. I am free from your criticism and I am free from your ridicule. I am free from your verbal and mental and emotional abuse because I am mature in him.

He recommends this prayer for times of trial: "Help me to not respond so quickly in my emotions and in my anger, respond so quickly in my foolishness and in my ignorance. ... Help me stop and pause and wait patiently, because you said that a patient spirit is better than a prideful."

Sheesh. Facebook and Twitter ought to incorporate those words in their sidebars!

In a way, if Hooks is right, social media is a non-stop stream of God getting our attention, because it is one endless deluge of controversy engaging us cognitively. At least, it *can* be, if we respond cognitively and patiently and lovingly, rather than just emotionally.

Hooks concluded with the following words of encouragement:

> Tomorrow, when the sun comes up, may your prayer, may your thought, be that you take the four corners of this day and shake out every blessing and shake out every pain—so that you receive the 'more' of God, the *pleroma* of God, and that that which the enemy would try to send to thwart God's plan over your life: that you see it, and you discern it, and you reject it and resist. ... I pray that you walk in the power that is yours by the adoption of sons, that you walk in the power that you can speak into an environment, and that it must change because the power of God that created everything around you is now in you, resting, and it abides. And if it is not in your heart, may it at least be on your tongue, and may you speak it with conviction so that the enemies of your destiny see that you are real and that you are strong and that you are mighty in Him.

Wow. I look forward to reading Hooks' poetry.

∎

Coffee Cake

I blame my aversion to coffee on my love for coffee cake.

Howzzat? Well, I'll tell you.

When I was four and five years old, my family lived in Sedalia, Missouri. In spite of the fact that we pronounced the name of the state "MIZeree" rather than the native-proper "miZURuh," if you get my drift, I pretty much thoroughly enjoyed my time there.

We didn't encounter tornadoes, but the frequent thunderstorms were spectacular. Summer nights would be spent lying on sleeping bags under the stars, watching meteorites and one spectacular supernova. Summer days were occupied with turtle trapping and crawdad hunting. There were church picnics, my first crush Joanie, and midnight frog-gigging.

I was introduced to the strange wonder of K-Jo Kindergarten, run by a couple funky ladies in a small countrified urban cottage. We adopted a stray tomcat we named Frisky. We made multiple trips on hot summer days to Johnson's Shut-ins, a natural waterpark of rockslides and swimming holes.

The trailer park in which we lived for a time was within walking distance of the county fairgrounds, and in 1967 the parks were overrun with hippies. It wasn't quite the Summer of Love yet, but they all nonetheless seemed terribly happy and affectionate, and I had no idea why.

Transistor radios blared "To Sir With Love," "I'm a Believer," "Happy Together," "Groovin'," "I Think We're Alone Now," "Incense and Peppermints," "Ruby Tuesday," "All You Need Is Love," "Brown Eyed Girl," and "Up, Up and Away." It was a great time to be a kid.

Oh. And there was coffee cake!

My mom was part of a gaggle of women who met weekly for coffee and conversation. Without fail, the coffee would be accompanied by what they called "coffee cake," made exactly the same way by whichever of the women was hosting on any given week. The Sedalia version of that delectable treat was made not with a uniform upper crust of brown sugar and cinnamon streusel, but with deep canyons of crunchy-gooey goodness swathed through a wonderfully moist yellow cake. And because I was not yet in school full time, I got to go along every week.

And have coffee cake.

Now, my very young brain made a logical but fatally incorrect assumption. I knew that chocolate cake was made from… chocolate; and I knew that apple pie was made from… apples.

It followed, therefore, that coffee cake must be made from… coffee. Right? After all, the ribbon of sweetness through the cake was the same color as coffee, right?

So the first time I tasted coffee, I was expecting…

You guessed it. The flavor of coffee *cake*.

Wrong! Ugh. What a rude surprise.

To this day I have not gotten over the bitterness of that disappointment.

But I still remember those coffee cakes. Mmmmm...

∎

Clarence Jordan

I recently of free-climber Alex Honnold's laser-like focus on his sport, "The appeal of being around a person like Honnold is obvious. Such single-minded devotion reminds us how passionless most of our lives are, and by contrast reminds us of what vitality can look like."

The same can be said about Clarence Jordan, whose name came up in conversation with church friends the other day.

If you've ever heard of Habitat for Humanity (and who hasn't?), then you know something about Jordan. For Habitat's founder, Millard Fuller, the appeal of being around a person like Clarence Jordan was obvious. Such single-minded devotion reminded Fuller how passionless and sterile most of our spiritual lives are, and by contrast also reminded him of what Christ-like vitality can look like.

After spending a good deal of time on Jordan's Georgia farm, Fuller decided to put his millions where Jordan's ministry was, and Habitat was one of the outcomes.

This topic is a timely one.

I was turned on to Fuller and Jordan by old friend Shari Kooistra, who lived and worked in Georgia for a number of years. While there, she consulted with Habitat for Humanity and visited Jordan's Koinonia Farm—where she learned the story of Clarence Jordan and shared it with Jenn and me.

At the time, twenty years ago, Jenn and I also were involved in a crazy-idealist experiment in communal living that bore some resemblance to Koinonia's early years. One big difference: Doulos, the house in which we lived, was based in a pretty comfy mostly white suburb south of Seattle. The biggest dangers we faced were rodents—and our own stupidity and selfishness.

Koinonia, on the other hand, was a real working farm in the Deep South during the fomenting years of the Civil Rights Movement. The KKK was active and aggressive and did not at all care for the Jordans hiring Black sharecroppers at the farm, much less sharing their dinner table and washrooms with them. Jordan was conducting about the most dangerously radical experiment in racial reconciliation and coexistence possible.

Reading about those years—and it was *years*—is greatly akin to watching Alex Honnold scale El Capitan without ropes… which he did for only four hours. Koinonia lived that dance with death for nearly a decade, surviving shootings, bombings, boycotts, and shunning.

So why I am I telling you about this? Because I was reminded of it the other day, and the comparisons to Honnold are striking. And because I keep forgetting that other people do not know about Jordan.

Which is not to adopt some White Savior superiority thing. John Perkins, Martin Luther King, Jr., Rosa Parks, Nelson Mandela, Paul Rusesabagina, Mahatma Gandhi—the list of people of color who have lived lives of great danger and peaceful protest goes on and on.

Clarence Jordan, by contrast, did not live life as a racial minority. But if you study the thoughts and actions of white Christians, particularly in this day and age, and then do a little reading on Jordan, you can definitely see that his understanding of what it means to be "Christ-like" placed him in a decided (if white) minority. He took Jesus' instructions to love enemies to an extreme and deliberately set about living in a manner that bore out The Sermon on the Mount as literally and faithfully as possible—something white Christians really need to look at a good deal closer.

It's a challenge I lay before anyone who thinks anti-violence is a "soft" form of Christianity. Read Dallas Lee's *The Cotton Patch Evidence*, and read Jordan's "Cotton Patch" translations of the New Testament. My bet is that, like me, you'll be wonderstruck at what you find.

Like Millard Fuller, you will likely find in Jordan a reminder of how passionless and sterile most of our spiritual lives are, and by contrast be reminded of what real-world Christ-like vitality can look like.

I dare you.

∎

Middle English

You all have Steve Escame to blame for this.

Part of College Prep English indoctrination at Foster High School included Scom's hazing ritual of *The Canterbury Tales*. It was not enough that we had to read the dang things, we also had to recite the opening of the *Tales* from memory... in proper Middle English.

> Whan that Aprille with his shoures soute
> The droughte of Marche hath perced to the roote
> And bathed evry veine in swich liqour
> Of which vertu engendred is the fleur

That's still from memory, forty years past, including the spellings—which are mostly right! And there was a lot more that we had to recite.

While studying English Lit at the University of Washington, I signed up to study Chaucer in Middle English a bit more—and ended up working with Associate Professor Míceál Vaughan on his textual analysis of ancient manuscripts of *Piers Plowman*.

How's that for obscure, and learnèd?

Middle English has never really left my blood. A couple years ago, I picked up a facsimile edition of the Tyndale New Testament—which is early Elizabethan English—and had such fun with it I decided to see if there were any Middle

English Bible facsimiles available. And behold! I found a hi-res PDF of the Wycliffe New Testament from about 1420. I bought it for myself for Christmas two years ago.

At first the Middle English text confounded me… and so I let it sit for a good long while. I had other things to occupy my time and attention. My long tour through the Tyndale, however, got me back up to speed with the Gothic "blackletter" script, and my confidence rose.

I've been reading the Wycliffe in the morning for the last few weeks. I started out by reading the text aloud out by the firepit in the afternoon sun, taking about thirty minutes to decipher my way through each chapter of Matthew. My pace has quickened quite a bit of late.

Last night I awoke with words in my head that I needed to write down. They went,

> "Every word that's sown holds promise of new light beyond these darkened days."

Or something to that effect. I felt that they were important somehow and that I should write them down—particularly since I never remember things like that from my dreams. But I was so out of it I couldn't drag myself out of bed. Instead, I lay there thinking the words over and over.

They were still with me this morning during my early work hours. By the time I sat down for quiet time and devotions, they were festering in me. I put them on paper and refined them a bit, trying to get closer to the "feel" of what they had meant to me during the night:

> Every word that's sown
> Throughout our fallow hours
> Holds promise of new light

One odd thing was that the words and the rhythms fit right along with a fragment of verse that I had scribbled during my week at the Spanish coast last month.

Odder still… when I set that aside and picked up Matthew Chapter 10 in the Wycliffe, I read:

> no thing is keverid or hid that schal not be schewid and no thing is pryvy that schal not be wist that thing that I seye to you in derk nessis seye ye in the light

That is, "Nothing is covered or hid that shall not be shown, and nothing is private that shall not be known. This thing I say to you in darkness, say you in the light."

Lo, the Scripture as translated 600 years ago said better than could I what my dream spoke in the dark of night.

Unreal.

■

Home

I greatly disappointed Jenn by never quite feeling at home in Des Moines.

Just before we moved in, she had hand-crafted paper decorations for four large die-cut pressboard letters that spelled H O M E. It was her hope that we would weatherproof them and mount them outside our front door. I demurred, and she was hurt, thinking that I found her creation ugly.

That was not it at all. But what it was... I could not put my finger on.

I know now. Even though I believed God wanted us in our Huntington Park home and had pulled cosmic strings to get us there, I never did feel *rooted*. Jenn and I enjoyed our best years in our gutted and made-over house... and it was a godsend.

But still... for as long as we lived there, I was always making plans to *get away* for one vacation or another. I told myself that it was all for Jenn, to give her things to look forward to and ease the pain and isolation of disability. But from the day we moved in, I think I felt in my soul that our stay was temporary.

The day that Jenn died, I took three long walks. It wasn't that I couldn't bear to be in the rooms where Jenn went cold; no.

That night, I had no problem sleeping in the bed where she had lived only eighteen hours earlier. The issue was: It was just time to be out. And still it took me six months to understand that I needed to move on. I needed to.

And just about the time I thought I was finding my place in the world, I stumbled unexpectedly across Twisp.

What is home? Home is where your heart is, they say.

Or, home is where you hang your hat.

Or, if you are Elvis Costello, "Home is anywhere you hang your head." Home isn't where it used to be, as the erstwhile Declan McManus sings.

Home is the place you don't want to leave; home is the place you can't wait to return to. When you have found home, you no longer think about what's on the other side of the fence, much less about the color of the grass over there. Home is enough.

For the first time in my life, I feel like I belong. It's good to know what that's like, and now I can always carry it with me—even if I choose to leave.

Home is the place you could leave if you had to... but if you did, you'd have no doubt that you'd be leaving it for love—real, true love—and you wouldn't have to live out your years wondering if that love were real.

Timing

Two weeks ago, I had an appointment circled on my calendar. I was supposed to be at a new friend's home at 7 PM.

> "Grace, my friends, demands nothing from us but that we shall await it with confidence and acknowledge it in gratitude."

At 1:30 that afternoon, I met another new friend for coffee, and my entire day veered off onto an unexpected lane. Just as I was about to leave for that 7 PM appointment, I was confronted with a choice: Should I stick with the original plan? Or make a new one?

A voice echoed in my head.

It was my own voice, parroting words I had written not long before: "A plan is just a framework on which to hang God's surprises."

God was most definitely laying some surprises on me December 1, so I decided to run with it. I changed my plans and jotted a quick apology to my formerly intended host.

> "Grace, brothers, makes no conditions and singles out none of us in particular; grace takes us all to its bosom and proclaims general amnesty."

How do we know the effects of such decisions? Did we make the right choice?

My good buddy The Shy Pilot has a field day running through endless what-if scenarios. Such mysteries are the grist of life, and sometimes we pummel ourselves through the mill with second-guessing and regrets. And the vast majority of the time we never end up finding out how things played out...

> "See! That which we have chosen is given us, and that which we have refused is, also and at the same time, granted us. Ay, that which we have rejected is poured upon us abundantly."

Well, last night, two weeks later than originally intended, I made good on that originally scheduled appointment. But the gathering was a little different. The invite list had changed, including a couple I met on that scrambled and rearranged agenda two weeks prior, and the purpose of the get-together had been reworked by my hosts.

Even the announced agenda for the evening had been jettisoned by the time we arrived. It turned out to be a dinner not unlike the climactic titular meal of Gabriel Axel's Oscar-winning Danish film *Babette's Feast*.

> "For mercy and truth have met together, and righteousness and bliss have kissed one another!"

The quotes in this essay are the words of writer Isak Dinesen, as delivered by the fictional General Lorens Löwenhielm.

Last night over dinner, mercy and truth met together; righteousness and bittersweet bliss kissed. Heartfelt stories of tragic loss and injustice intersected in improbable and glorious fashion and were bathed in prayer.

And the stage was set because, over the course of a fortnight, the universe hung a few surprises upon my plans, the plans of my hosts, and the plans of others with whom we broke bread. If divine appointments exist, surely this was one.

I cannot say more, because only my story is mine to share; but take heart. Listen to the Spirit which guides you, and have confidence in it.

This is what the universe asks of us: to believe, and then act on that belief—not because we know we are strong, but because we know we are weak, and that we are in the hands of a mighty God who loves us. In spite of our pain and sorrow. *Because* of our anguish.

And through the wounds which are also our healing.

Merry Christmas, all ya'll. Hallelujah!

■

Lewis & Clark

I was truly wonderstruck when I first read the journal of William Rogers Clark in the fall of 1971.

I was already a pretty nutty nine-year-old, writing in my "Childhood Memories" book that I wanted to be not a fireman, policeman, or cowboy when I grew up, but an archaeologist or paleontologist. I could draw several species of dinosaur free-hand and knew more than was good for me about King Tut, the excavation of Troy, and the poor grotesquely captured souls of Pompeii.

But a visit to Fort Clatsop at the beginning of a long summer road trip with my family began my next obsession, the history of exploration. I sped through the one book my parents bought me about Lewis and Clark's quest for a Northwest Passage through the Louisiana Purchase and then picked up Clark's abridged journal when my mom was done with it. (She was a voracious reader in those days!)

During the fifth-grade year that followed, I made a diorama replica of Fort Clatsop for a class assignment and then launched into the biggest craft project I had yet undertaken.

Sometime when I was seven or eight years old, I had become proficient in decoupage, "the art of decorating an object by gluing paper cutouts onto it," as Wikipedia tells us today. I was either expert enough or ambitious enough by the time I was nine to decide I could tackle something on a grand scale:

a five-by-four-foot scale replica of a map of Lewis and Clark's journey.

I first salvaged a piece of scrap plywood from my dad's shop and cut it to size on our rickety belt-driven table saw.

Just picture a runty little kid boy-handling a large sheet of plywood through a noisy antique blade on a dark winter night, and wonder to yourself under what sandpile my parents' heads were buried. I imagine I did most of this kind of work while being "supervised" by my sister Elane or some other babysitter. In what household would a parent hear the whine of a saw in the basement and not wander down there to see what's going on?

The plywood then had to be prepped for decoupage, which involved patiently filling in knotholes and splits with resin, then sanding the patches smooth. Then the entire surface was "antiqued" with the aid of a blowtorch, carefully scorching (but not burning!) every square centimeter of wood. A burnt odor was pretty pervasive in this step... and remember, that was twenty square feet of scorching! Yep.

I created the map itself out of a large sheet of butcher paper. The Thorndyke Elementary "opaque projector" threw an image of the source map onto butcher paper tacked to the school's wall, and I sketched the outline of the map and expedition route in pencil.

The map-to-be then went home with me, where I painstakingly translated the pencil marks into permanent-marker detail and drawings. (I had not yet graduated to calligraphic pens, nibs, and India ink.)

The finished map was then "aged" through techniques I had already mastered from "treasure map" making—solutions of coffee grounds brushed lightly over the paper, then littered with the contents of moist tea bags, carefully wiped away after a precise length of saturation. As the paper dried, it had to be pressed so that it would not wrinkle.

The map was then rolled and its edges burned as a finishing touch.

Decoupaging such a large sheet of paper requires great patience, as the process is not something you get a second chance at. You are either 100% successful with placement and avoidance of air bubbles, or you fail completely. I had put way too many hours into this project for failure! I used a system of strings and paperclips to keep the paper suspended above the plywood as I slowly laid it onto the gluey surface, inch by inch, over several hours.

To preserve the work, the top of the paper is also decoupaged (the step where I would find out if my permanent inks were really permanent!) and then hand-waxed.

These days, I don't know if I am more dumbfounded at my nine-year-old self for conceiving and completing this project, or at my mom, who has kept this map through move after move for nearly fifty years! I came across it again in my folks' basement the other day while looking for a bottle of wood glue to repair a dining room chair at their house.

Will wonders never cease?

Mushing

A week piloting a dogsled in Alaska's Brooks Range north of the Arctic Circle was by far the hardest thing I have ever done—physically *and* mentally.

My adventurous friend David Stark and I booked ourselves an early spring mushing trek in 1994. Just after we made our final payment on the trip, we went to see the Disney film *Iron Will*, about an early twentieth-century mushing race in Minnesota—which turned into a desperate survival struggle for its young protagonist.

We left the theater literally sick to our stomachs.

If that's what dogsledding was like, this would be the biggest mistake of our lives.

Sourdough Outfitters, in the remote outpost of Bettles, just south of the Gates of the Arctic National Park, was our base of operations. The first afternoon we received orientation and training on how to harness and drive our team of eight dogs.

We were led by outfitter Brandon Benson, who owned the dogs, and Iditarod veteran and champion Bill Mackey on a short out-and-back "fun run." It's all about framing the dialogue, right?

I fell—and fell *hard*—eight to ten times during that four miles of "fun." In one desperate incident, the dogs slung the sled full speed over an embankment onto a concealed icy roadway. Caught completely off guard, I launched from the sled in midair, lost my grip on the handlebar, and came down hard right in the middle of the road. The sled only stopped because it wrapped around a tree off the trail on the opposite side of the road.

After the training run, I could barely move.

Given that we expected to do twenty or thirty miles a day on this trip, I quickly calculated that, at my current fall rate, I would bite the dust fifty or sixty times each day... for nearly a *week*. Something had to change. I very seriously considered pulling out of the trip.

Even before hitting the trail, I was confronted with a most difficult proposition. Quit, or adapt?

During that sleepless night at the Sourdough lodge, I replayed those four miles in my head over and over. *What was I doing wrong?* What could I do to correct it? Trail conditions were so bad—icy and constantly slanting left and then right—that I was having a very hard time keeping my weight over the "proper" foot while shifting positions and braking.

I concluded that, to survive, I needed to stop trying to use my left foot to brake—throwing proper instructed technique right out the window. I may be somewhat ambidextrous with my forelimbs, but that left foot... no coordination whatsoever. If I tried to do this sport "right," I wasn't going to make it. Plain and simple.

With trepidation, I committed to setting out for six days on the Arctic trail.

My improvised footwork actually worked. I "fell" only once on the first day, on a steep slope where three teams all went down together in a horribly tangled, sliding mess of slush, harnesses, sled runners, and gnashing teeth... canine *and* human.

The eight sled teams of our entourage were spread out over a mile or so of trail, each of us traveling with a certain autonomy. At one point, as we were cruising at ten miles per hour or so over a long, straight stretch of open trail, I noticed Dave's lead dogs charging up behind me... *and start to pull out to pass on the virgin snow to my left!*

What was Dave thinking???

Well, he was probably thinking, "How did I manage to fall off the sled?"

There were Dave's eight dogs just running to kingdom come, and they weren't going to let me stand—or run—in their way.

All I could think to do was what I had seen in ridiculous old Westerns: As Dave's lead team inched past me, I leaned waaaaayyy out to the left to grab their harnesses! The stunt actually worked, and I slowly braked my sled to a halt. Dave's dogs had the courtesy not to try biting me, and Dave soon jogged up, out of breath and sweating heavily.

The only damage I sustained that day came earlier. We had passed over a spot where snowmobilers had built a fire in the middle of the trail—a four-foot-deep hole straight down to dirt, eight feet across. Thinking the hole was just another fun roller-coaster dip, I let my team of dogs hit the hole full speed—and broke a rib when my chest hit the wall on the far side while jumping up out of the hole while still clinging to the sled behind the leaping team.

But I didn't lose the sled... I just got dragged behind it for a couple hundred yards while I caught my breath, clinging desperately to the handle of the sled as my knees and feet jangled painfully over the concrete-like broken ice of the trail. I eventually managed to pull my knees up onto the runners of the sled and then regain my feet.

But technically, that was not a fall!

Every day of the trip contained similar misadventures—like the third day, when I punched my shoulder through the three-inch ice on the Koyukuk River on the way to Dead Man Pass. For stretches of several hundred yards, the trail was the frozen river itself, and managing the team was pretty tricky. Too light a foot on the brake and you'd start coasting past the dogs as they sensed a slack lead line; too heavy a foot, and you'd tire your team. Naturally, I didn't have quite the hang of it, and when I tried to correct a slack line I ended up like a plumb bob oscillating at the end of a string. The runners caught in an ice ridge as I swung hard left, and down I went. I gritted my teeth in the ice shards but held my sled firm.

That night, in a relatively swanky trapper's cabin that another group had abandoned because the trail was too rough, Bill and Stumpy Jim (a Missouri trapper who ran snowmobile support for the group) regaled us with tales of Arctic sled-dog disasters. Dave and I had probably mentioned *Iron Will*, and they were not interested in having Minnesota tales outdo Alaska. Bill, in particular, relished recounting the loss of a musher and team of dogs who had broken through the ice on the aptly named Wild Lake.

Perhaps he was pulling my leg; but the fourth day, as Brandon and Jim were occupied with snowmobile repairs, Bill led the client teams out to... Wild Lake.

When we reached the turnaround point, three of the teams, including mine at the rear, elected not to follow the lead of Bill's team and instead plunged over the lake's embankment and headed out onto the ice.

The reason I was pulling up the rear was that I was by far the heaviest of the mushers, and while my team was plenty game, they were in no way up to breaking trail with my load on board.

The two teams ahead of me kept moving nicely on the surface of Wild Lake and executed a nice little loop as Bill called to the dogs from the bluff above. But my poor dogs moved increasingly slower, and when they noticed that they were the only team left on the lake they simply stopped.

Gradually, my sled started sinking backward into the slush and soft snow covering Wild Lake, the rotten ice creaking frighteningly beneath me. I didn't dare step off the runners, so instead lay sideways across them, paddling frantically with my hands and feet to try to provide some jump-start momentum for my tired dogs. I even resorted to the cardinal sin of mushing, launching a profane stream of curses at my dear mutts. Bill chastised me for this later, after my team eventually got moving again, but he was still smiling from the ridiculous sight I made at Wild Lake. And Bill was probably thinking that his story-telling stunt couldn't have worked out any better!

On day five, the first leg of our return trip, Bill led us on a side trip up Michigan Creek over fresh trail—the best mushing of the trip. We nonetheless had to twice—four times, actually, counting the return trip—jump holes in the ice over Michigan Creek... scenes straight out of *Iron Will*, including the one where Will's dad dies. Yipes!

On our final day, my sled suddenly jammed its runners in ice, and I launched in a flip over the handlebar, landing squarely in the sled's basket just behind my wheel dogs, Fax and Digger. Boy, were they surprised to see me.

Dave described the week's experience as similar to playing a full game of tackle football... without pads, every day, for a week.

Sometimes the sleds were canted at a 30-degree angle—or more. I remember at one point literally riding the sides of the runners. And the pitch would change constantly, switching rapidly from right to left and back again, all while moving at ten to fifteen mph. Rarely a moment to just stand still and ride.

By the final day, I was so sore and having such a hard time breathing I spent six hours repeating to myself, "You can do this! You can do this! You can do this!" I have never been as mentally exhausted as I was upon our return to Bettles.

After the trip, Dave and I rented *Iron Will* to see it again.

Reaction this time? "Piece of cake."

Sometimes you don't really know what you're getting yourself into… but you also don't find out what you're made of if you never try anything difficult! You may just be very surprised by what the universe has in store for you.

■

Scott Hicks

A society that no longer values or heeds prophetic voices—words spoken to hold us accountable to our principles, ideals, and calling—is ill indeed. And prophetic voices who still themselves in times such as these because speaking out has actual consequences will have much for which to answer.

I have been consistently impressed since I first ran across Scott Hicks on social media a couple years ago. Scott's treatise on the nitty gritty of immigration law went viral in the wake of President Trump's January 2017 travel ban—and not because of the kind of vitriol which has become *de rigueur* in this day and age but because of its sane, rational, and detailed exposition of actual fact.

Scott is a full-time immigration lawyer and part-time pastor at Oregonia United Methodist Church in Lebanon, Ohio. As both a pastor and an attorney working to help immigrants and asylum-seekers work their way through our legal system, he stands at a unique position at the crossroads between compassion and the law.

And as he stands for both the law of Christ—that is, the law of love and grace—*and* the laws of the land, he advocates both for "doing things the right way" and doing things a more right and more just way.

As a prophetic voice, he functions in a number of valuable ways.

On social media, he relentlessly sheds light on truth via facts and details which our media are either too lazy to report or too biased to reveal. And he does so in a consistently non-hysterical fashion through both modeling Christ-like behavior and moderating discussions that are respectful and civil. If you want to keep abreast of what's happening with the legal ramifications of various issues related to immigration, you can do little better than following Scott's fact-finding and reportage, which often highlights the real-world experiences of his clients and colleagues.

And he has voluntarily taken on this role at great cost to his personal life, because he perceives the cultural value.

At the same time, given his intense familiarity with our legal system, Scott calls upon our government—the executive and legislative branches, and law enforcement agencies—to cease their partisan bickering, blatant disregard for existing law, and frequent outright hostility toward those who see our country as a bright hope for *their* future.

How disheartening it must be to have the city on the shining hill of your dreams kick you in the teeth.

Finally, as a pastor, he calls on the Church to be the Church in deed, not just in theory. As he explains in a YouTube video,

> We've lost the biblical narrative of how God looks at foreigners and how God looks at our obligations to foreigners. And we've allowed it to be swallowed up by political sound bites and we've allowed it to be swallowed

by fear—and the fear has been absolutely pervasive since 9/11.

And when you look at it and you start to think about it, God specifically says "I am not a God of fear," and perfect love casts out fear. And so we are a people of grace; that is the entire essence of who we are as Methodists and as Christians.

We believe in the grace of God and the love of God and so we have an obligation to live out our lives not in fear but in grace and in love—and we have an obligation not to exclude people, not to shun people, not to try to kick people away. We have an obligation to include and to welcome and to shelter.

And so that's to me the faith that we hold and God is demanding of us.

A people who no longer values or heeds prophetic voices—words spoken to hold us accountable to our principles, ideals, and calling—is ill indeed.

Listen to what Scott has to say. Spend some time reading what he writes. Absorb a little of how he lives, and the principles and ideals to which he is committed.

And after his prophetic voice has rubbed you the wrong way a little, ask yourself: Isn't that what a prophetic voice *should* do? Shouldn't you want God nudging you, even goading you toward positive change?

Don't you want to be a little less stiff-necked every day?

Even if you don't quite see things the way that this prophet does, aren't you just a little wonderstruck at his calling and his faithfulness to it?

And finally, ask yourself: Have you allowed your own prophetic voice to be stilled, or to be drowned out by the cares of the world?

■

Gregory Boyle

Boyle is a messenger, but he is not the Message.

Still, Father Gregory Boyle's particular message is this: God's compassion is boundless; we would all do well to model it.

Boyle's 2010 book *Tattoos on the Heart: The Power of Boundless Compassion* came to my attention while I eavesdropped on conversation between Molly Lachapelle and Bonnie Stevens. They're book people and were comparing notes on latest reads prior to a screening of *The Face of Winter* at The Barnyard Cinema.

A Jesuit priest, Boyle has been working in LA's "gang capital of the world" for three decades as founder of Homeboy Industries. The ways in which he has seen lives transformed are endless, and *Tattoos on the Heart* collects some of those stories—which read like twenty-first-century parables.

Saturday, I read the following:

> The Beatitudes is not a spirituality, after all. It's a geography. It tells us where to stand.
>
> Compassion isn't just about feeling the pain of others; it's about bringing them in toward yourself. If we love what God loves, then, in compassion, margins get erased. "Be compassionate as God is compassionate," means the dismantling of barriers that exclude.

> In Scripture, Jesus is in a house so packed that no one can come through the door anymore. So the people open the roof and lower this paralytic down through it, so Jesus can heal him. The focus of the story is, understandably, the healing of the paralytic. But there is something more significant than that happening here. They're ripping the roof off the place, and those outside are being let in.

I had the chance to talk about Boyle and his mission and his vision for compassion with Dale and Sue Peterson after a church supper on Saturday night, and passed along information about the book to Dale. I also mentioned it during Bible study at Winthrop Friendship Alliance Church yesterday morning.

And then, this morning, what do you know? The next passage in my morning Bible reading is... Mark 2. In Wycliffe's Middle English, the intro to the story is worded like this:

> It was heard that [Jesus] was in a house, and many came together so that the house took not them, neither at the gate. ... And there came to him men bringing a man sick in palsy. ... When they might not bring him to Jesus, for the company of people, they made the roof naked where he was, and making open, they sent down the bed.

As Boyle likes to emphasize, a hurting person's first exposure to compassion is like having the roof ripped off, of your very self being laid bare.

Being on "the inside," though, is of no use if you're not actively engaged in tearing down walls, says Boyle, and I agree. And it necessitates coming down off your high horse, requires abandoning the ivory tower, means leaving behind the land of theory and breaking through the illusion that we are somehow better than others.

"Compassion is not about the relationship between the healer and the wounded. It's a covenant between equals," Boyle writes, a "shift from the cramped world of self-preoccupation into a more expansive place of fellowship, of true kinship" which is "the truth of how closely bound we are together, dissolving the myth that we are separate at all."

The stories that Boyle tells—the parables that he relates—about Dennis and Anthony, about Matteo and Julian, about Memo and Miguel, and about so many others… well, if you want your heart to remain stony and cold, don't look them up.

If you want to rip through some of your roof, though… it's time to get on board.

In "Ink Blots," I wrote:

> Somewhere in a pearlescent pool hell
> An angel sports tats on its wings
> Surely there is encouragement
> In being desperately human
> In the fellowship of natural flaw
> Birds of a feather, you might well say
>
> Yet we do not consider equality
> A gift to be cherished
> Instead conspiring to be gods
> At least dawning celestial forms
> We ink wings on our lats

Cinemetastasize angels who long to feel
We self-justify as we are
Err-apparent to the Divine

Yes, somewhere out there, we fancy
An angel sports tatted wings
When folded they depict
An atlas of the mortal form
The weight of the heavens
On its bare and blotted shoulders

Boyle is convinced he works with angels… which is a word that might also be translated "messengers."

I think he's right.

■

1 + 1 = 3

I posted the following on Facebook in June 2017:

> Craziest thing in the world happened yesterday afternoon.
>
> On the way to meet Elane and my mom and dad to celebrate my folks' 80th birthdays, Jenn and I stopped at B&E Meats in Des Moines to pick up some potato salad. Because it was a busy afternoon for B&E, I had to park in front of Flora Laura.
>
> On the sidewalk in front of the florist shop, Laura had an "antique" bike parked. As I was pulled the car to a stop, I remarked to Jenn, "Hey—that looks just like my old bike. Same color scheme and everything!" I looked closer, and it was even the same brand and make: a Raleigh 3-speed.
>
> After I picked up the potato salad, I took a closer look at the bike because it had a custom headlight generator on the rear wheel, just like the one I had put on mine, one I had as a hand-me-down from my brother Bob.
>
> Wait…This wasn't *just like* my old Raleigh… it *was* my old Raleigh!
>
> The only bicycle I ever owned, which I rode all over Tukwila, Riverton Heights, McMicken Heights, Seatac, and Des Moines.

Laura's sister Julie Rex Linehan, an old friend of ours, was inside the shop with her baby Poppy and told us that Laura had picked up the bike at an estate sale just a few weeks ago.

When my parents shipped that bike to some thrift store around 1986, I of course never expected to see it again... much less just down the road from where I live. Crazy.

Okay. Ya wanna talk crazy? Really?

Just this morning, I had the opportunity to relate that story—as part of a much larger, even more unbelievable story—to an old friend, Erin Nayak. But I *did not reference the Facebook post*. Or even give her a thumbnail of the story. I just sent her a link to my writeup of the full story *on my blog*.

Half an hour ago, I received a notification that a complete stranger had "liked" this June 2017 post on Facebook.

It's possible, I suppose, that the Internet is smart enough to scan links in PMs, connect the text of an independently hosted eighteen-month-old blog post to an eighteen-month-old FB post and then decide to show that eighteen-month-old post to a random stranger on FB, who then presses the Like button.

But, wow. When a post about really odd coincidences gets resurrected so oddly after all this time... well, it sure gets my attention.

■

Acceptance

Several times in recent weeks I've had the opportunity to tell people about the amazing transformation that came about in Jenn during the final years of her life.

The change began in April 2009 with a dynamic spiritual encounter with God; but the work didn't really come to fruition until Jenn accepted one of the hardest things for her to believe: that disability was a life-ending reality.

Key to helping Jenn leverage her spiritual epiphanies into transformational change was the tandem of a "Spiritual Formation" program and therapy with Dr. Lisa Day of Meier Clinics.

Lisa first encountered Jenn in group therapy sessions stretching from 1994 to 1998 and was instrumental in guiding Jenn to the equine therapy program for eating disorders at Remuda Ranch in Arizona, which Jenn went through in 1995.

Later, as Jenn was completing her group therapy sessions in 1998, she would come over to my Bothell carriage-house apartment on Tuesday nights, after leaving group therapy, and we would practice the communication and coping techniques she was learning from Lisa. So I knew all about "Dr. Day" long before I met her.

When Jenn needed to dive back into therapy in 2010, she turned once more to Lisa for one-on-one work. This time around the big project was helping Jenn grieve the loss of all her "nevers"—never being able to work again; never being able to eat a normal dinner; never being able to get her Master's degree; never again being able to memorize lines for theatrical productions; never being able to write the books she wanted to author; never being able to swim or soak in a spa; never having the strength, stamina, or sturdiness to raft the Grand Canyon again or go backpacking; likely never living to see fifty years old, much less make it to our 60th anniversary as she had promised herself, or take care of our parents in their old age.

So much loss.

During these years of therapy with Jenn (and in the years since) Lisa was working on her forthcoming book *The Art of Grieving*. I just listened to a podcast this afternoon in which she talks about the central concepts she taught Jenn during her last years and which brought Jenn to the place where she could truly invest herself in the lives of others.

"In the twenty-five years that I've been a therapist," says Lisa, "what I find as one of the most common things that comes in my office is the statement, 'I can't believe…' And that can be anything from 'I can't believe I didn't get the job,' 'I can't believe my boyfriend had an affair on me,' 'I can't believe my dog gets hit by a car.'"

Lisa certainly heard plenty of that kind of talk from Jenn over the years. The nevers were overwhelming, and Jenn just couldn't believe that all that had been taken away from her, yet left her cripplingly alive.

"That's prohibitive to moving into the coping process," Lisa explains, preventing people from "integrating things that they are powerless over" into their actual lives. The language itself, she has found—the very words, *I can't believe*—triggers "a stress response, which we all know is going to trigger the release of cortisol," the fight-or-flight hormone.

The words we use can either help, or they can hurt… and in this case, "when we come in fighting a reality, it complicates the coping process, it complicates grief."

As she did with Jenn, Lisa counsels patients to change their language to modify the chemistry of the response. For example, if you find yourself saying, "I can't believe that I just got fired!" you bring yourself to the place where you can say, "I accept that I just got fired."

Sound trivial?

Try it sometime. It's not at all.

Through long practice I've trained myself to say something like, "I can't believe that idiot just cut me off! … Well, okay, I *can* believe it, because it just happened." And then I feel the stress just ebb away.

The upside to this whole process—and this is where Lisa's therapy came in to touch so many other people through Jenn—is what it does in transforming a person's life. The body's internal chemical response to *I can't believe*… "hardens the heart," Lisa says, "creates a bitterness, it creates a resentment. Which in my opinion interferes with our ability to have compassion, to have empathy, to be able to have greater room for love."

When acceptance found its way into Jenn's life, when she finally accepted that all the nevers were reality, when she let go of all the bitterness and resentment, she truly began investing selflessly in others.

When we come to the proverbial "Y in the road," Lisa points out, "and we say, 'Do I have influence here, or am I powerless?'," the ability to accept difficult realities allows us to "invest our emotional resources where we do have power."

If you knew Jenn during the last years of her life, you saw this at work in a huge way… in spite of the rib fractures, in spite of the seizures, in spite of excruciating pain in her hips, and, finally, in spite of hospice. Jenn exited this life giving away every last bit of herself that she had to give. She ceased thinking of life as a thing to be grasped. She let go, and gave to others.

If you experienced her generosity, and I know many of you did, you were no doubt wonderstruck. It was a thing to behold.

∎

The Road Taken

Yes, that's a Robert Frost reference.

I was watching a documentary called *Minimalism* on Netflix the other day and was completely taken aback to hear former Wall Street financial analyst A. J. Leon describe his life-changing epiphany.

Having selected a career in finance and accounting on a very pragmatic earnings-potential basis, he applied himself to his work and before long was making a six-figure salary with hefty bonuses and a corner office. At year's end 2007, his boss called him into his office with the offer of a lifetime.

"This was the gamechanger," says Leon, who would later found Misfit Inc. "This was me being a junior partner in this firm—and everything that I'd ever worked for was going to be handed to me. Right then and there. In banking terms, I was 'minted.'" The moment everyone dreams of, right? Success on a platter.

And it was so surreal that Leon felt like he was floating outside of himself—like it was happening to someone else. "I walked out of his office and I walked back into my own, and I closed the door behind me... and I just started weeping. Because I realized I was completely and utterly trapped, and that I would never be able to walk away from that amount of money. Any dream that I had of living a life of purpose and meaning, and being an adventurer, and somebody that would actually take risks and live a life that is deliberate and intentional—those were gone."

The wheels started spinning really fast for Leon. Everything was on the line. "I don't want to be *him*," he thought, seeing in his mind's eye the successful junior partner who just left his boss's office. "I don't envy his life. Maybe this was never for me to begin with. And maybe, if I don't leave now, I'm going to be that dude for the rest of my life."

So he packed up his belongings, walked into an elevator, and descended twenty-eight floors to embark on the "road less traveled."

Now, the reason Leon's tale struck me hard was that it so closely mirrored my own similar epiphany in 1997. The details differ; but I had also just "won" an astounding corporate "victory" that was the culmination of career ambition. I also was making six figures, plus incentive stock options, and was next in line for Director of Engineering or a V.P. slot. And *I* went home the night of that triumph and wept uncontrollably. Because, like Leon, I realized that "success" had "trapped" me on an ever-accelerating treadmill, doing work that did almost nothing to feed my soul. The cost was just too high.

I didn't walk off the job, as Leon did. But I charted my exit strategy nonetheless.

Was it to be the right choice? Would the road less traveled be the right one for me? Or would *my discarded engineering career* be Frost's "road not taken," the one which I would some day regret leaving behind?

Well, this is actually where my story gets interesting. A full year ahead of time, I set my "early retirement" date as Thursday, June 18, 1998. The next day, June 19, I would board a plane for Scotland, taking my sister, Elane, with me for a two-week jaunt. I told no one at work about my plans but set about tying up twelve years' worth of loose ends—and bit by bit handed over the reins to my competent Leads.

About eight weeks out from End Game, I decided I ought to finally let management know. I walked into the office of Quinton V.P. Ed McCauley, who was my supervisor at the time, and started to tell him that I would soon be leaving.

Ed held up a hand. "Don't say another word," he said with a characteristic wry smile. "I think I know where you're headed. So I'm going to tell you something I probably shouldn't.

"The company is about to be acquired by a venture capital group, and there will be a layoff. We don't know when it's going to be announced yet, but it's coming."

I told him I was puzzled about why he was telling me this. "If you quit," said Ed, "you'll get nothing but your walking papers. If you wait, I will put you on the layoff list. Severance packages will be very generous." After all we had been through over the years, I guess Ed felt like he owed me a huge favor and probably an apology for his early lack of faith in my vision for the Engineering department.

Since he asked me not to tell him more about my plans, I honored the request and didn't. I just figured everything would shake out prior to June 18. If it didn't, I would simply work my final day on June 18 and hand in my resignation the morning of June 19 on my way to the airport.

The weeks raced by—too fast. Not a peep about layoffs was heard.

By Monday, June 15, I was getting really nervous. By Wednesday, Jenn was having a hard time talking me down from the stress. By then, I should have been telling my employees about my departure and making sure they all had what they needed to pick up where I was leaving off.

Thursday, June 18, was the longest day on the job in my life. Every moment of every hour was a nauseating churn. And when I left work that day, I was truly lost. I got home and packed my bags and sat in silence, staring out the dark windows of my Bothell apartment.

In the morning, I loaded my bags for the drive to the airport. As I arrived at Quinton to hand in my resignation, even in the parking lot I could feel that there was stress in the air.

As I walked in the door, someone—I can't remember who—swooped in to inform me that I was wanted in Ed's office.

June 19. It all came down the day I was scheduled to leave the country, on a trip planned a year beforehand! June 18 had been my last day on the job after all.

After meeting briefly with Ed to confirm what I already knew was happening, I was escorted by security back to my office to collect my personal belongings. With a loaded cart—and a six-month severance check—I was sent packing to my parking spot.

I was allowed to say goodbye to no one. Not a soul. As far as anybody knew, I was simply "expendable," *persona non grata*.

On the way to the airport, I stopped by Children's Hospital to visit Jenn at work. We prayed, and I again wept. I really had no idea if I was doing the right thing.

It turned out I sure was.

Dunno if I chose the "road less traveled," particularly, but the road taken certainly did lead, to use Leon's words, to "a life of purpose and meaning, and being an adventurer, and somebody that would actually take risks and live a life that is deliberate and intentional."

Now, I personally don't believe there is any risk involved in living the life you were meant to live. But this road I have taken?

I have never, ever, regretted it.

■

The Gutter

You can't make this stuff up.

After I returned from a snowshoeing slog through deep powder off Poorman Creek Sunday afternoon, I stopped by the post office to pick up my mail. I hadn't been there in several days, so I thought it was high time I checked in.

Since it was a Sunday, I was naturally the only one to park at the curb that afternoon. When I returned to my car with the mail, I was watching my feet carefully, as the sun had been out and the snow/ice mix at the curb was treacherously slick.

While fumbling with my keys, the corner of my bifocaled eye caught a flash of silver in the slush clogging the gutter. I shifted my head slightly so my lens would allow me to focus down there.

Sure enough, a solitary earring, sporting two drilled stones, was drowning in the chill. I stooped to pick it up and examine it.

This was hand-crafted stuff, almost certainly sterling. I've seen enough jewelry here in Twisp of late to start telling the difference.

I considered going back inside and tacking the earring to the bulletin board; but the odds of reconnecting this lost item to its owner that way were a billion to one, I thought. Whoever lost it would have no idea where to begin searching and would probably never think, "Maybe I should check the post office…"

So I pocketed the earring and thought I might as well get it to one of the local smiths so the silver content could be reclaimed.

I know several silversmiths these days, oddly enough, including Kelleigh McMillan, whose studio is at Twispworks, and Sarah Jo Lightner, whose work can be found at the Methow Valley Jeweler's Collective, among other places. I had been in meetings with both of them just a few days ago.

Right at the end of the block where I live, though, is Nicole Ringgold Jewelry Designs. So when I walked into Twisp yesterday, I took along the earring—but with the President's Day holiday, the shop was closed.

Today, then, when I walked to the Methow Valley Community Center for a committee meeting, I stopped by to see Nicole.

"What's new?" she asked as I closed the greenhouse door behind me.

"Well," I replied, getting right down to business, "I found this earring." As I dug into the change pocket in my jeans, Nicole's expression became oddly intrigued in a way that took me aback a bit. Like she already knew what I was going to say.

"I found it in the gutter and thought I ought to give it to you so the silver could be reclaimed." I produced the earring and handed it to Nicole over the display case.

"You found this?" she asked, wide-eyed and smiling.

"Well, yes. In the gutter. It's silver, isn't it?"

Nicole didn't answer my question. Instead she said, "This is mine."

"It's yours?"

"This is my earring." And she didn't merely mean that it was one she made and sold to someone else.

"This is from my favorite pair of earrings."

"You're kidding," I replied, dumbfounded.

"No, I'm not. I lost it a few days ago and have been beside myself wondering what happened to it." The joy and wonder on Nicole's face were amazing.

What are the odds? The things that the universe wants to return to us… wow.

Years and years ago, Jenn and I collaborated on a web journal called "After Eden." The essays we wrote and edited were inspired by the words of G. K. Chesterton. "The world is in a permanent danger," he wrote in the Introduction to *The Defendant*, "of being misjudged."

Bear with me as I offer here an extended sequence of quotes from Chesterton as he explains what he means. It's important.

"The two absolutely basic words 'good' and 'bad,' descriptive of two primal and inexplicable sensations, are not, and never have been, used properly," he writes. "Certain things are bad so far as they go, such as pain, and no one, not even a lunatic, calls a tooth-ache good in itself; but a knife which cuts clumsily and with difficulty is called a bad knife, which it certainly is not. It is only not so good as other knives to which men have grown accustomed."

Think about that for a moment and ponder all the things to which we apply the word "bad."

"The coarsest and bluntest knife which ever broke a pencil into pieces instead of sharpening it is a good thing in so far as it is a knife," continues Chesterton.

> It would have appeared a miracle in the Stone Age. What we call a bad knife is a good knife not good enough for us; what we call a bad hat is a good hat not good enough for us; what we call bad cookery is good cookery not good enough for us; what we call a bad civilization is a good civilization not good enough for us. We choose to call the great mass of the history of mankind bad, not because it is bad, but because we are better.

Or so we believe.

This is truly countercultural thinking, from well over one hundred years ago.

But what does this have to do with Nicole's earring? I'm getting there. And so is Chesterton.

> Now it has appeared to me unfair that humanity should be engaged perpetually in calling all those things bad which have been good enough to make other things better, in

everlastingly kicking down the ladder by which it has climbed.

If we think we are standing on the top rung, he means, it is silly for us to demean the other steps which led us to such supposed heights. He instead calls for a different way of thinking.

> I have investigated the dust-heaps of humanity, and found a treasure in all of them. I have found that humanity is not incidentally engaged, but eternally and systematically engaged, in throwing gold into the gutter and diamonds into the sea.
>
> I have found that every man is disposed to call the green leaf of the tree a little less green than it is, and the snow of Christmas a little less white than it is; therefore I have imagined that the main business of a man, however humble, is defence. I have conceived that a defendant is chiefly required when worldlings despise the world.

You cannot see the world properly if you despise it, even certain parts of it.

But the world can amaze you if you expect to find jewels in every corner. And this, my friends, is precisely what led me to Nicole's earring many, many years after the publication of "After Eden."

Inspired by Chesterton's vision, I have also made it my business, both literally and figuratively, to investigate the dust-heaps and gutters of humanity, as well as its loges and board rooms. You never, ever know what wonders you are going to find.

I read just last night about one of the ex-gangbangers who works with Father Gregory Boyle (about whom I have written earlier). He orients fellow homies on his work crew by telling them, "All of you are diamonds covered in dust." He chokes up when saying this. "You can wipe your dust off here."

Sometimes we help others reclaim what they have lost—figuratively, perhaps, or even literally, as I did for Nicole this morning.

Sometimes, though, we just need a mirror held up to our eyes, so that we can find ourselves in the gutter to which others have cast us—or see, from the depths of the sea in which we drown, that "we live amidst a universe soaked in grace that invites us to savor it," as Boyle writes.

Diamonds and gold… and silver, indeed.

Everywhere.

In everybody.

Wonderstruck.

■

Virtual Friends

"Where are the strong?" I quoted Nick Lowe a couple days ago. "And who are the trusted?"

Sometimes you find those stalwart friends online.

A year ago, Mark Allen Sommer and his wife, Julie, visited Seattle so they could be on hand for Jenn's Celebration of Life, even though Mark had only met Jenn—or me, for that matter—once in person, after a lecture I delivered at Notre Dame.

But Mark knew Jenn, and knew her well. The three of us had bonded deeply via the Internet.

At the 2004 One Ring Celebration in Pasadena I devoted an entire presentation to documenting the power of the web to help forge friendships every bit as "real" and vital as those we make in other spheres of life. My relationship with Mark is one of those examples, as is the friendship I have found over the years with Dawn Doughty Davidson, whose artwork I discovered online and whom I recruited to create the images for *Two Roads Through Narnia*, which Jenn and I published in 2005.

This morning, Dawn wrote a very moving tribute to another virtual and vital friend, Laurie Draegeth, who died young and tragically.

"Laurie and I met online via a now-defunct fantasy art site called *Elfwood*," Dawn writes.

> "I posted my first awkward bits of Prydain fan art there, and she popped out of the faceless crowds when one of my images made the front page. I wish I had saved that account, now; wish I could go back and find those first comments of hers that alerted me to a kindred spirit, a spark flashing across space, bright against the dark sea of cyber-passersby."

A spark flashing across space, bright against the dark sea of cyber-passersby. Oh, my.

Over the span of more than a decade, Laurie and Dawn only met once, cementing their bond during a week's visit at Dawn's Florida home. Dawn continues:

> It was Laurie whose friendship taught me that those on opposing ends of the political and religious spectrum were not the ogres I had been brought up to believe they were, but could be—shockingly—mere fumbling humans, as well-meaning as any of us can be, groping into the infinite, thoughtful, who had reached different conclusions about this world and the next. I don't always know what to make of this change in my own perspective anymore, but I do know it has made me a more compassionate and humble person—perhaps more Christlike, ironically, than I ever was, back when I knew everything.

Back when I knew everything. I remember those days, too—and so does Mark. Whatever else one might say about the Internet and even social media, those who have ears will hear... and grow, from whatever valuable source one may find.

> There is no blueprint for losing a 'virtual' friend—dear God, what a term, as though the people you interact with every day online are somehow not real, not flesh-and-blood friends just as solid as the ones you can put your arms around, whose loss is just as heart-wrenching and shatteringly permanent and unbelievable and impossible.

Laurie became a virtual friend for me, too, through her online banter with Dawn. And no loss is virtual.

"This isn't a tribute as much as a recording," Dawn concludes.

> My work is my real tribute to her—the fan work she loved and was such an integral part of, and the original work she was so pleased, on my behalf, to see gaining in success. She'd tell me, with her usual frank pragmatism, to suck it up and keep working, that life happens and it's up to us to take it as it comes, to live as full as we can and not waste the time. It is certainly how she lived her life, unaware of how little time she had.
>
> It doesn't feel real, still, and maybe it never will. The other oddity of a friendship being long-distance: that gut-punch of the departed not being physically present isn't there; I could pretend, perhaps, that her phone is dead, that she's taking a social media break, that my life hasn't changed in any practical way.
>
> But it has. There's a void now, a silence that used to be filled with her commentary, a missing heart on a post she would have loved, a last message left unread. Posts I made in the interim, as I blithely enjoyed my life, while she was

gone and I didn't know it yet, seem insulting to my own sensibilities now... that I was enjoying anything in a world with a Laurie-shaped hole in it that I somehow didn't feel all the time. Until I did.

But the world moves on, joy and pain intertwined. That is the paradox of our existence, the puzzling, tear-stained, love-filled debate between mind and heart and spirit.

Thank you, Laurie, for the beauty and wonder you brought to this life. For being one of the strong, one of the trusted. And thank you, Dawn, for these words.

And for your virtual, virtue-filled friendship.

The Infinite

Because the universe wants us to be surprised, to be in awe of what comes next… and how could you not be?

Sunday night and Monday I watched *The Fault in Our Stars*, which came at me out of left field.

The title of the film is taken from Shakespeare's *Julius Caesar*, as Cassius is persuading Brutus that the Senate needs to take matters into its own hands. If our present is not what it needs to be, says Cassius, don't blame it on fate; blame it on ourselves, for not doing the most we could with what the Universe gave us—for accepting less than what might be. Of course, Cassius is trying to foment assassination, but that's beside the point! (Or perhaps the point is outside the plot. Whatever.)

Monday morning, I had a long talk with my oldest friend, Stephanie Cortes. We've known each other for more than fifty years, having bonded in second grade. While talking about her children, Erica and Jake, Stephanie mentioned the magical feeling that a mother gets while holding a sleeping infant—a sensation I obviously will never know.

But I did mention that it must be a little like what I felt when watching Jenn sleep, which I did a great deal over the years due to Jenn's prolonged illness and her plague of narcolepsy. On vacations, in particular, I would often rise early just to read and watch Jenn sleep. Her waking hours were filled with so much pain and limitation; but while she slept, so beautifully and peacefully, all things were possible.

She never recalled dreaming, but I often wondered what went on inside her head during those hours. "I think there's a poem there," I said to Stephanie.

My brain went to work.

Wednesday, after a 2.5-hour call with my colleagues Rick Stevenson and Max Losee about the future of our video journaling company, StoryQ, I wrote the following:

> In 1977, space probe *Voyager* began its journey out of the Solar System.
>
> In addition to its scientific mission, *Voyager* was also an ambassador of the Human Race, carrying with it a "golden LP" of data representing the best that Earth had to offer: photos, greetings from the United Nations and President Carter, the cries of whales and babies, works by Mozart and Chuck Berry, indigenous world music, and spoken words in fifity-five languages.
>
> If alien life finds that golden disc millennia from now and comes to Earth to investigate, what will they find if we are no longer here? What legacy will we leave? The slime trail left by social media and political pundits? What will there be to say, "This is who we really were"?
>
> Can there be a *more* golden record of our race? We say, yes. Yes, there can be.

There can be the Human Record, a central repository of every living person's story captured privately and securely on digital video and salted away for posterity. No human left behind undocumented. No life lived in complete obscurity. Every birth a miracle, every story a treasure. Every person an eternal interstellar ambassador.

We are the Virtual *Voyager*.

Limitless possibilities.

Thursday morning I sat down to pen a poem titled "Strachur Entreaty," a riff on watching Jenn sleep in the living room of the gatehouse at Scotland's Strachur Estate the morning of Boxing Day in 2002. The piece invokes Hamlet's soliloquy, in which Shakespeare uses sleep as a metaphor for death: "to sleep, perchance to dream."

And the final line before the poem's postscript echoes the metaphor, calling it "the rite of infinite possibility."

Last night, after a longer than usual day of work, I sat down to see what was in my queue on Netflix. At some point I had bookmarked the William Shatner documentary *The Truth is in the Stars*, a musing about the connectedness of all things in the Universe. Shatner's quest here is to find meaning in his *Star Trek* legacy, as he drives toward a climactic meeting with Stephen Hawking.

As is the case with most of Shatner's documentaries, it's a fascinatingly rambling mess of a film. Shatner is a riveting bundle of cultural contradictions, famously reclusive and gregarious in the same breath, tongue-tied yet verbose, more at ease with horses than he is with human beings.

I actually fell asleep during Shatner's talk with Hawking. "Well, that figures," I thought through my drowsy fog.

To sleep, perchance to dream.

I woke in time to hear Shatner describe his time with Hawking as visiting "with a Holy Man," and intone to Hawking, "I would love to stay for dinner."

After a brief patio interlude outside Hawking's home, the film concludes with Shatner on a punt in the Cam River pondering his place—and our place—in the cosmos.

The final line of the film: "The truth is not in the stars, but in the minds of the people who imagine a future of infinite possibility."

How extraordinary that my week should conclude with those words.

Extraordinary.

Wonderstruck.

Perchance to Wake

In my dream, I was best man to a cad—a fact I knew through long experience.

But hey. He was *my* cad.

The night of the wedding rehearsal was as you might expect, given that we were all in our fifties, married, divorced, or widowed. We were giddy enough over the occasion, and liquored enough, to be close to riotous but mature and disillusioned enough to riot with restraint.

In my dream, the bride was my ex-fiancée.

As effervescent as ever, she was the life of the dinner and of the party… in spite of the best efforts of my buddy, the groom, to upstage her.

The revelry in the hotel ballroom wound down and the ladies retreated to the rooms to prep for the bachelorette party which was to be held in the adjoining spa and sauna. Boys being boys, even if graying, the bachelor party got in its first and second rounds in the ballroom before retiring to the bar.

Just as we were migrating in that direction, the women blew through the middle of our party on the way to the spa. They were now all stripped down to hotel robes and bare feet.

My heart ached as the bride swept past, catching my eye.

Oh, how badly I wanted to tell her that this was all a mistake, that the groom was a fraud, that he was not at all the man she thought he was.

But how could I say a word? Even a sane person would think I was just spewing sour grapes, my broken heart simply wanting to shipwreck these other passers in the night upon the same rocks which grounded me.

And so I bit my tongue and simply watched as she passed through the double doors with her maids.

Then she turned, caught my eye again, let the left side of her robe fall open to the waist. And smiled.

■

I woke with a palpable jolt and a gasp. The dream was simply too real. It did not feel at all like the many cinematic dreams I have. I was not in the dream, as I usually am, a character whom I am watching remotely. In this dream, it was all from my point of view, all seen through my eyes in a single take, as they say in the biz.

And the thing was, I really *did* have an ex-fiancée… the very one in the dream, a woman I began dating in the aftermath of my late wife Jenn's passing.

As the day wore on, I just couldn't shake it. I was rattled. I had not spoken to my ex in months and, as we had an almost non-existent circle of mutual friends, I literally had no idea what was going on in her life. Since she had not only broken off the engagement but asked me not to contact her, I had worked very hard to honor her desires.

Finally, though, I sat down at the computer that afternoon about 4:00 PM. I Googled her blog... and the featured image on the top story was a photo of her ring finger sporting a very large engagement stone. The text, written just a couple weeks prior, announced that she was indeed engaged to be married.

Whoa. I did not see *that* coming.

One of the things she had told me when we broke off our engagement was that she could not possibly marry a man she had only known for six months. No matter *how* well she *felt* she knew him. And she had known this fellow less time than she had known me!

Against the desires of a whole lot of flashing lights and warning klaxons in my brain, I sent a simple email that said, "Congratulations! I saw your blog today. Best wishes!"

Less than thirty seconds later, she replied with a subject line: "Hold That Thought."

Incredulously, and with the hair on the back of my neck standing up, I opened the email and read:

> I broke off the engagement yesterday. God has shown me that my fiancé is a fraud, and is not the man that he has been passing himself off to be.

■

Although I did share the basic content of the dream with her later that evening, I did not go into detail. It was enough that I explain the timing of my contact and the reason for it.

And, as you might expect, she took the dream as divine confirmation of what she had already sensed. I know, right?

No, we did not get back together. We did not even meet, just a brief chat on the phone and a Google Hangout or two. After taking some days to catch up on things and talk through the circumstances of our breakup with the benefit of some distance, we parted ways again, a little more mature and a little more healthy.

I do not expect to see or talk with her again.

Then again, I did not expect that dream. Much less for the dream to essentially be true.

I do not put a lot of stock in what I expect!

■

Joy

Two years ago, toward the end of Jenn's eighteen months of psychogenic seizures, I loaded her into a borrowed wheelchair to attend a "meet and greet" VIP event with the band Switchfoot at the Showbox Sodo in Seattle.

During the photo op encounter, Jenn rose from her wheels long enough to share her butterfly story with the band and stamp their wrists with butterflies for the night's performance.

In brief, this is what she told them: Jenn was delivered from depression when a butterfly landed on the scabs of her slashed wrists on September 24, 1994, and licked her wounds for forty-four minutes. A real miracle, witnessed by more than a dozen women.

About the encounter, Jenn wrote:

> In the group photo the VIP photographer took, Drew has pulled his sleeve up to show the inside of his wrist. I asked each one of the men if I could stamp a butterfly on each of their wrists; each one accepted (even requested!) the mark. I told them to watch the mail for something with butterflies for them & their wives. Can't wait to send them some personal notecards—and include the story of my Hope in the form of a butterfly.

P.S. Also, as Greg notes, these men are the real thing—more than I expected. I know that [for a band like Switchfoot] there is a necessary persona that is well-honed by now, but to see Drew SHOWING OFF his stamped wrist is indicative of the sense of personal interest they've cultivated *sans* completely losing any ties to reality or their constant giving of themselves even in a two-minutes handshake and snapshot.

It IS all about HOPE!

Switchfoot's latest album *Native Tongue* was released not long after Jenn's passing. "Joy Invincible" was the first song from to really grab me, for obvious reasons. What lyrics!

> Tears were in my eyes when the phone rings
> If only life didn't need us to be this brave
> But we don't live in the world of if only's
> Stretched tight in between our birth and our graves
> Hallelujah nevertheless, was the song pain couldn't destroy
> Hallelujah nevertheless, you're my joy invincible

I already had a ticket to the April 11 concert at Seattle's Neptune Theater when I heard the song... but I figured I needed to do the meet-and-greet with the band again.

"You may remember meeting my wife Jenn two years ago," I began. "She asked if she could stamp butterflies on your wrists before the show." Drew immediately perked up. "There was the story about the miracle with the butterfly, right?" Yes, there was.

I told the band that Jenn felt bad about never making good on her promise to send their wives a gift before she passed away. But I still passed on her story of Hope—a volume of *Taking Flight*, Jenn's collected poetry which I published for her posthumously.

I thanked the band for their music being such a balm through Jenn's long illness, for helping Jenn "see the way home," to quote a lyric from the most recent album. Jon Foreman hugged me, and thanked me for the poetry.

During the concert, I really broke down during "If the House Burns Down Tonight." This was one of Jenn's favorites, from 2016's *Where the Light Shines Through*.

"One heart, two hands, your life is all you hold," Jon sings. To "hold, hold tight and let the bitter go" became Jenn's final project. "Yeah let it go, and give me the fire."

Switchfoot performed "Joy Invincible" on Thursday night, for only the second time during the tour. So fitting. It felt like a tribute to Jenn.

To a certain extent, I feel like I'm falling in love with my late wife all over again. What a fine thing!

∎

Destiny

"Well, I always wanted to be legendary!"

I would most often trot out this line with Jenn when the odds were stacked against us, such as being 1000 points in the hole while playing Pinochle with my folks—or when Jenn would happen to be whupping my backside at Nertz or Casino. (But never Mario Kart, for the record.) I believe I even employed the phrase a time or two when the situation with Jenn's health seemed particularly dire, and we needed God to pull out a stop or two to get us through the crisis.

Behind both the jest and the dead seriousness of this declaration was the idea that brilliant comebacks are only possible when the odds are longest... as when Judah Ben-Hur gets chained to an oar in a Roman trireme.

I first saw *Ben-Hur* on the big screen when I was six years old at the Lewis and Clark Theater, just a block and a half from where I grew up, during its 10th anniversary re-release. I am almost certain that this film—and others like *Doctor Zhivago* and *Lawrence of Arabia*, which my parents also took their impressionable children to see—shaped my passion for the dramatic arc of fate.

I suppose that it makes sense that I saw *Ben-Hur* on the big screen again last night, precisely fifty years later, with Stephanie Cortes and her older sister Anita. Bob, Elane, and I all delivered newspapers to the Cortes residence at one point or several, and Stephanie and I met for the first time fifty years ago when I got moved up into the second-grade class that we shared with Erin Bader and several others of our Foster High graduating class of 1979.

If you're going to watch sixty-year-old films, you might as well do it with great childhood friends!

The technical achievement of the chariot race aside, and regardless of many brilliant choices with shot composition and *mise en scene* ("Help him! He spoke French!"), the film's script, which was doctored by Gore Vidal among others, is steeped with references to the strange ways in which our lives can often seem orchestrated.

"It's a strange destiny," says Ben-Hur, for example, at a reception in Rome, "that brought me to a new life... a new home." That line certainly resonates with my move to Twisp, which has seemed both fateful and extraordinarily strange. But this sense of destiny, inculcated in me at an early age and promulgated through long practice and a form of positive reinforcement, also begs certain questions.

Like, "Why does Jesus give water to Judah Ben-Hur, but not to others?"

Or, "Why does Judah get his chains loosed in the sinking galley while other slaves remain shackled and drown?"

Or, "Why do Miriam and Tirzah get healed from leprosy while others do not?"

I have of course struggled with answers to questions like these over the years. In the context of the movie, the answer is: "Because this is Judah's story—about the miracles necessary in his life… the particular means that God used to reach Judah's heart and renew his mind." If we listened to someone else's story, the details would be completely different… and the story might involve a painful, lingering death like Jenn's rather than improbable acts of heroism like Judah's.

Either way, you get legendary.

And, frankly, Jenn's story is more compelling than Judah Ben-Hur's.

The universe does want to surprise us… each one of us. And it knows what each of us needs to be restored to awe.

Even if that moment of restoration must come as we step out of this life and into the next.

■

The Millionaire Waltz

> Bring out the charge of the love brigade
> There is spring in the air once again
> Drink to the sound of the song parade
> There is music and love everywhere

I have always loved Queen's "The Millionaire Waltz," from the 1976 album *A Day at the Races*—which is packed wall-to-wall with the band's trademark bombast and sentimentalism.

As Jenn and I long ago began planning our wedding, originally scheduled for July 1, 2000, I envisioned choreographing a waltz to the song for our first dance.

When we moved our wedding date up to August 22, 1999, the planning timetables were suddenly and dramatically shortened. I never got around to the choreography, much less even mentioning the idea to Jenn.

> Come back to me, how I long for your love
> Come back to me—be happy like we used to be
> Come back, come back to me
> Come back, come back to me
> Oh, come back to me, oh my love
> How I long for your love
> Won't you come back to me?

"The Millionaire Waltz" has always stuck with me, though, and hit me particularly hard this morning. For forty years, the song resonated with my own sense of the melodramatic; but I couldn't really appreciate the sense of loss expressed. In fact, quite the opposite.

Even in the darkest hours of Jenn's prolonged illness, I was profoundly conscious of the great privilege it was to be at her side throughout it all.

> Give a little love to me
> Take a little love from me
> I want to share it with you
> Come back, come back to me—make me feel
> You make me feel like a millionaire

Still.

Wonderstruck.

Jon Kottwitz

I made a blind leap from the Boeing Military Aircraft Company to Quinton Instrument Company in 1986.

I'd been working in missile systems since graduating from the University of Washington in 1984 with a degree in Computer Science, and both the work and the workplace were becoming toxic to me. I honestly didn't care where I landed, and rather than do an exhaustive job search "the usual way," I hung my shingle with a contract house and took the first placement they offered.

QIC pretty much hired me simply on the basis of my resume, though of course I did do cursory interviews with Software Manager Tom Masters, Engineering Director Chuck Orrestad, and project Software Lead Tom Pierce.

In 1986, it was pretty easy to get hired in the industry based on your BS in CSci. (I imagine you get my drift.) But I was good, and QIC was a good fit. I sailed through my three months on contract working alongside fellow new contractor Jim Wootten and we both promptly became direct hires at the contract's conclusion.

The brain trust of the Q5000 Stress Test Monitor team was the aforementioned math major Tom Pierce and electrical engineer Jon Kottwitz. After my discovery of "The Heyman Uncertainty Principle" (which is in itself a whole 'nother story), I began working closely with Tom and Jon in debugging the Q5's assembly code. Those few shorts weeks in 1987 were the most invigorating of my engineering career.

The chemistry between Tom and Jon was electric. Not only were their individual skills dynamic—Jon could multiply hexadecimal figures in his head with 100% accuracy—but their brains completely complemented each other. They completed each other's sentences in a weird leap-frogging sort of way that made the jump from A to Z by frequently leaving out entire sequences of letters along the way. I managed to contribute in significant ways, I guess, mostly by staying out of their way but adding key bits of insight when it mattered.

I also contributed heavily to Tom and Jon's extracurricular studies in "stochastic methods"—code for "playing cards." The three of us partnered with QA engineer Randy Walls in epic lightning-fast lunch games of four-handed Pinochle. We even hung around after work to play from time to time—a tradition that got cut short when recently promoted Engineering Manager Ron Stickney caught us playing cards in his office.

Vic Pipinich, Jim Wootten, and a rotating cast of other engineers soon joined us for monthly poker games at my house—hours-long marathons that we continued for twenty years, right up until Anthony King's seriously untimely death in the wake of brain cancer.

But I'm getting waaaaayyyy ahead of myself.

It was in the purely social setting of those early poker games that Jon and I discovered our mutual love of Spaghetti

Westerns. I now find it hard to believe, but I had barely known Jon a year by the time we were saying, "I bet we could make our own Western."

By the summer of 1987 I was working with Gretchen Sass and Mark Stevens on a storyline for what would become the script for *Who Shall Stand*.

For location scouting, some combination of Mark, Jon, and I visited just about every ghost town, abandoned cabin, and defunct stamp mill and mine in Okanogan County. The burgeoning storyline centered around horse thieves, desperadoes, and miners… so locations included the interiors of one-hundred-year-old mine shafts. Some of the exploring we did was simply insane.

But it was inspiring! I camped at Spectacle Lake for the week of Labor Day that September and hammered out a script. During the days I would tramp around the primary "set" at Nighthawk, jump in the Similkameen River to cool off from the 100-degree temps, and then spend evenings sitting in front of my green-glowing Kaypro II CPM OS portable PC at Spectacle Falls Resort working out plot and dialogue between Sim Richards, Pine Martin, Cletus Hanks, Thomas Fewkes, Boudreaux, and The Pinkerton Man. Best week of my life to that point, I think.

Jon was set to co-produce the film with me. Over the winter, I worked on storyboards with DP Mark Stevens while QIC's tech (and production sound engineer) Steve Bevens worked on music themes for the score, and we recruited buddies from work to round out the cast. Tom signed up as Boudreaux and started studying the French Canadian accent while John Faytinger, Rolf Bergstrom, and Tim Malone joined the cast. I brought in my old college buddy David Stark and new acquaintance Chris Chesser as ringers, and a summer 1988 shooting schedule was set.

And then Jon's marriage broke up, and he decided to join the Peace Corps. Two years in Botswana, starting in late April.

WTH???

I completely respected Jon and his decision, though. The man was principled, and he knew his life needed redirection.

To help send him off properly, Tom and I treated Jon to dinner at our favorite downtown Seattle eatery, Thai Palace, and rigged a Pinochle deck so Jon could leave on the high of a 1500-trump hand.

Yes, Jon, that hand was rigged. After thirty years, it's time you know.

We corresponded with Jon during his years in Botswana, and when he returned we added him to the Q4500 project, which I was managing. He remained part of the absolutely fantastic Engineering Department at QIC—with which I worked until I left the company in 1998.

After I left, the QEPC—Quinton Engineering Poker Club—continued to meet, and I officiated at the weddings of many former Quinton co-workers… including Jon and his new bride Pam!

Together, they started a new family and now have seventeen- and nineteen-year-old sons.

And now Jon, too, has been struck with brain cancer. Symptoms developed with alarming rapidity in May of this year, and by early June Jon had been diagnosed. A large tumor was removed at Swedish five weeks ago, and he is now in rehab, trying to relearn use of the left side of his body, as rounds of chemo and radiation therapy are set to begin next Monday.

Jon has been strong and capable all his life, glad of the opportunity he has had to be of help to others. He is not used to needing help with routine functions or delving into the realm of faith, and is desperate for a miracle.

So many things are new to him now, including prayer—something he really wants to become comfortable with.

I love this man. Love him deeply. He has always left me wonderstruck.

■

Coincidence

"What do we say about coincidences?"

"The Universe is rarely so lazy."

I have finally been driven to write about *Sherlock*, the Cumberbatch-Freeman take on Sherlock Holmes and John Watson—simply because these Season 3 words between brothers Mycroft and Sherlock provide me with an utterly suitable variation on my Wonderstruck tagline.

If the Wonderstruck column had existed in March of 2018, which it did not, I probably would have written this column then rather than a binge-watch review of the *Sherlock* BBC series for South King Media. But I had not yet been quite pushed over the edge, though Season 4 of *Sherlock* was certainly nudging me that direction.

My original notes about the series appear in my journal on the backside of the page containing my notes about *Wonderstruck*. Small wonder.

"I'm a high-functioning sociopath. Do your research."

I am what they call a "late adopter." That is, I usually "come to the party late," leaving others to fight their way through relentless hype (and disappointment) about whatever the latest "thing" might be, whether the iPhone, Adele, Ed Sheeran, or... *Sherlock*.

My resistance to the latter broke down rather more quickly than most of my irritating biases because of my interest in Benedict Cumberbatch. While Jenn slept during a flight to Scotland in 2012, I snuck in the first half of Episode 3, "The Great Game," from 2010's Season 1. The opening scene, in which Holmes impatiently corrects the grammar of a prospective client in a Belarus jail, immediately reeled me in.

> "Stay away from Sherlock Holmes."

I was hooked, though I wouldn't get around to watching much of anything of significant length for a good long time. Funny how caring for a desperately ill wife can take up a lot of attention.

I did manage to absorb the first two full seasons somewhere during the first half of this decade, though I can't recall when. I know I certainly enjoyed them… but when I finally ran across Seasons 3 and 4 early last year, after Jenn had died and I was working my way through her journals and poetry, prepping them for publication… well.

And to hit Season 4 Episode 1 right after the memorial service… huh.

> "In saving my life, she conferred a value on it. It's a currency I don't know how to spend."

Am I any swifter on the uptake than Sherlock? I don't know. I'd like to think that I spent the currency of Jenn's love pretty well through the first part of 2018.

And I'm convinced Jenn was shepherding me through that transition.

Sherlock did, too, among other stellar entertainments like *Wonderstruck* and *Detectorists*. The tears that poured out of me in March 2018 were copious and profound.

> "My old life… it was full of consequences."

All of that led more or less directly into my serendipitous encounter with the Methow a year ago, and my sudden, unexpected transition from West Side to East.

And now, after a year in my new home, I decided to screen *Sherlock* again after a very disappointing string of cable TV offerings. I won't name names, because I really have no interest in slaying other people's sacred cows… but I really longed for something smart, well-made, and thoroughly engaging.

So here I am plowing my way through the series again, mining memorable quotes that read like a roadmap through my wonderstruck life.

> "When does the path we walk on lock around our feet?"

I wrote down the following final quote while watching the show last year, but I can't dig up the source. Maybe I'll run across it in the next few days as I work once again through Season 4. Or maybe I won't… because maybe it wasn't from the show. Maybe it was from me, inspired by the show.

Or maybe it was from something else that the universe placed in my path at just the right time.

> "Grief is a gift from God to remind us of our love."

∎

Brian Tittle

Who is Brian Tittle? And what does he have to do with McDonald's? I shall tell you.

I attended the forty-year reunion of the Foster High School class of 1979 on Saturday night. I have stayed in touch with a number of my classmates over the years and also made it to the 15th, 25th, and 30th reunions—so I wasn't surprised at seeing the vast majority of the sixty or so attendees.

I'm also fairly active on social media, so there were several folks there I hadn't seen in forty years who I was glad to find on hand—but nonetheless "made sense" being there: Steven Lang, Paul Dillinger, Deborah Bradley Mays, Sensei-Alex Thomas, Michelle O'Brien, and Mike Anderson, among others. After all, I'd at least exchanged a message or birthday greeting with almost all of them at some point in recent years.

But Brian Tittle…

Thank God for name tags, cuz if I'd passed him on the street I would not have recognized him. Or he me, most likely, as we have both gone the balding-and-goatee route.

"I have more of a chin now!" he declared, a sentiment I echo.

Brian, Tim Stevens, Jim Moore, and I spent a ton of time together our senior year in high school—the last three months, particularly. Due to quirks in our schedules, we all ended up in the same pre-lunch Study Hall period with Mr. Tobin our final trimester—and within three days, we had driven him so crazy with our short-timer rowdiness that he told us just to leave and never come back. Thus it was that we ended up with a two-hour lunch every day for eleven weeks.

Despite the "closed campus" policy in force at the time, we liberated ourselves daily—and the spring weather of 1979 cooperated nicely. Our most common lunch destinations were McDonald's... and Burger King, which at that time was running a "free Whopper" punchcard promotion. Buy ten, get one free.

Well, we, um, somehow acquired one of the special burger-shaped punches and a stack of cards, and proceeded to rotate our lunch visits around the various South Seattle Burger King locations for a non-stop string of free Whoppers. After three or four weeks of that, we actually got sick of Whoppers. (Saturday night, Brian said he thinks he still has that punch stashed in some box of miscellany!)

Yes, we were ethically challenged, believing at the time that we were "flexing our creativity," or something like that. In retrospect, I find that a good deal of senior-year creativity was channeled into various nefarious activities... But a lot was also channeled into Sue Pike's second-year Spanish class, which Jim, Brian, and I were in together. Along with Terri (Haggerton) Woyvodich and Claire Foster, we staged some outrageously funny stunts as part of class assignments.

One of them—which I had forgotten about until talking with Brian and his wife, Carrie, Saturday night—involved helium balloons that McDonald's had recently started giving away.

Brian, Jim, Claire, and I had elected to stage a Spanish-language version of "The Three Little Pigs"... but instead of acting it, we opted for puppets. At lunch, prior to class, we loaded up Brian's car with McDonald's balloons; and then, crouched behind up-turned desks converted to use as the puppets' "stage," Claire voiced the wolf while Brian, Jim, and I did the entire sketch breathing helium for squeaky pig voices. I'm not entirely sure we actually finished, due to the laughing that ensued.

Following that, we upped the ante with a rewrite of "Snow White and the Seven Dwarfs" as the Spanish equivalent of "Black Rain and the Seven Perverts." This was a revamped tale of a prostitute (Black Rain, played by Terri) banished into the woods by a jealous Madame (played by Claire). There, Black Rain runs across a band of merry pimps, with whose help she returns to the city in a challenge to the Madame—who sees Black Rain not as a threat to her beauty, but to her physical endowment.

"Quien es mas grande que yo?" she exclaims in front of the mirror. "Who is bigger than me?" And with that, Claire thrusts out her chest in a vigorous and buxom display. This performance was captured on reel-to-reel videotape and never got old.

The Gang of Five's efforts culminated with a fifteen-minute Super-8 Western called *Llamarada Gloria*, patterned after the short film *Blaze Glory*—itself a sendup of melodramatic tropes. I played the titular sheriff (who passes his spare hours playing Russian roulette... solo) while Brian, Jim, and Terri portrayed bandits intent on mayhem. After a botched attempt at blowing up the bank's safe (a scene involving black powder, matches, and nearly burning down Tukwila's former schoolhouse and library!), the trio kidnaps the mayor's daughter (Claire)… and Llamarada rides to the rescue.

The climax of the film was staged atop boxcars along the Duwamish River. Other locations included trails at the Schoenbachlers' now-vanished dairy fields near Southcenter and the sand pits up at The Loop on 158th Street.

None of us was really a good enough student of the language to pull off these improvisational assignments directly. We were aided by underclassman Mayra Aquino, who had recently relocated from Puerto Rico with her family. I would write a script in English, then rough it out in what we called "Foster Spanish"—a sort of pidgin in which "Latinized" English would suffice when we didn't know the actual words. Mayra would then clean things up into proper Spanish—and we would simply memorize the lines, often without really knowing what we were saying. Mayra had her fun with this, taking advantage of our ignorance, as Sue Pike can attest.

I'm really not sure how much actual Spanish we learned through all of this—but that was the most fun I ever had in any class. My mind's eye is full, in particular, of Brian's expressions and body movements when he performed. A naturally expressive guy, he nonetheless took things to a whole new level with unique characteristic mannerisms and vocal inflections.

I spent some time last night trying to compare his delivery to various actors and comics… and came up empty. A pint-sized Christopher Lloyd, maybe? Brian was one of a kind.

And to be honest, he was such a crazy and wild cat that I never expected to see him again—either because one of the schemes he and Dan Wright concocted would prove fatal, or because he would simply disappear to the Congo or Colombia and never return.

Running into Brian last Saturday was so unexpected, and so delightful, it literally made my month!

"Sue Pike gave me a D-minus in that Spanish class," he told me. "But she refused to fail me.

"'Your Spanish is terrible,' she said, 'but I've never seen anyone work so hard.'"

Or have so much fun.

■

Denise Driscoll

The world needs more people like Denise.

Two years ago—hard to believe—my wife of eighteen years, Jenn, was starting into her final decline. She opted for hospice care on September 15, 2017.

In parallel, one of the miracles of social media was taking place. As Jenn's condition worsened, the network of friends around both of our Facebook accounts widened, and warmed.

Soon that net drew in an old, old acquaintance—Denise Driscoll, Foster High School class of 1978. I was class of 1979, which has always been super about staying in touch with one another. So good, maybe, that I often end up forgetting who was class of '79 and who was class of '80 or '78.

At any rate, at some point Facebook's friends-of-friends suggestions connected Denise with me. I certainly remembered her from high school, so that was a no-brainer. What surprised me was the easy empathy with which Denise connected to Jenn, who was a complete stranger to her.

Denise simply decided that Jenn was important to her because Jenn was important to me. She not only followed Jenn's spiral toward her demise, consistently offering words of wisdom and comfort, Denise also became truly engaged with the copious amounts of information I shared in the months following Jenn's death and leading up to Jenn's celebration service the following March.

Denise was living in Colorado at the time Jenn died... so all of this connection was happening remotely, exclusively through Facebook. At one point, Denise lamented the lack of hiking chums where she was living—so I told her I would be happy to slog through the woods with her, if I happened to be handy, come her next birthday... even if it meant tramping through Colorado snow. This promise was definitely presumptuous, given the extreme level of inactivity I'd been experiencing for the last decade or so!

By January 2018, Denise had in fact moved back to the Seattle area—so we met for a six-mile walk along the Cedar River to celebrate her birthday. I was wearing a brand-new pair of sneakers and developed about the worst blisters I've ever had. Smart move.

A month later, we met for a steep walk in the Cougar Mountain trail network. By then, I had started walking regularly, trying to get back in shape again and lose weight, and—believe it or not—trails with elevation gain of 800 feet were just about my limit. Or so I thought.

It was a good hike that day, but Denise was clearly slumming. I, on the other hand, had been too aggressive with twenty to thirty miles of walking each week—and during the downhill stretch that day, I felt my left knee protesting loudly. I doubled down and just upped my daily dosage of ibuprofen instead of taking the rest my knee was telling me it needed.

Two days later, my left MCL popped while on another hill climb... and I was completely out of commission for ten weeks while I rehabbed.

As my summer progressed and I slowly regained my ability to gain (and lose) elevation while I walked, Denise began acquiring other hiking partners... and in a big way! Since the middle of last year, she has regularly scheduled a series of hikes all over Western Washington, reconnecting with several of her 1978 classmates. She has been instrumental in bringing all of them back into the outdoors, out of varying degrees of isolation, and helping them regain their stamina and physical health.

And Denise is not some professional athlete or seasoned trainer; she's just a decent person with a highly developed sense of compassion and a love of the outdoors. A love she enjoys sharing.

Her love of the outdoors includes annual participation in beach cleanups on Earth Day, intense shepherding and training of her nieces in the ways of the natural world, and engagement with various conservancy efforts.

Her compassion has lately overflown in stepping in to coordinate tracking of all the loved ones lost in recent decades by alumni of Foster High School. There's so much passion and sorrow attached to that Facebook group—and Denise has just plunged right into the middle of it, generously and warmly.

I have been thinking about writing about Denise for a long time, because when I first got to re-know her she was mourning a great many broken things in her life. When she was between jobs, I really felt like this was a woman who seriously deserved some blessing.

As I have seen blessing not only flow into her but out from her as it multiplies, I have really been in awe.

Finally, a couple of days ago, I concluded, *Geez, that's it. This woman needs a little PR. She's amazing.*

Real friends. This is what can grow out of social media, folks.

The world needs more people like Denise. And you know what? It's gonna get them. Because you can be one, too.

Be like Denise.

∎

Patience

I grew up with a legacy of great anger, handed down through the Wrights from generation unto generation as violence begat violence.

Granted, my version of the family curse was greatly watered down from the fist-fights that my grandfather shared with my great-g, and the worst that my own father indulged in were childish temper tantrums.

But patience... oh, my, but I had very little, as any family member who ever watched me learn to tie my shoes or ride a bike or swing a croquet mallet could attest.

Being a hyper-self-aware child, I knew that I had no desire to replicate my father's tirades (or my own mallet-flinging) as an adult. So at age twelve or thirteen, I set out to do something about it.

A couple of years prior, family friend Roger Roll, aware of my rather prodigy-like expertise with woodburning and leathercraft (and that wall-sized Lewis & Clark map I wrote about earlier!), had given me his personal collection of calligraphic tools, and I was soon immersed in the world of India-inked lettering.

The really demanding part of any calligraphic project was the sheer inability to correct mistakes. Everything had to be planned out and done right the very first time.

So, knowing I needed patience—and being absolutely enthralled with *The Lord of the Rings*—I decided that I would replicate the Middle-earth map on 11 x 14 parchment paper.

For practice, I started with Thror's map from *The Hobbit*, basically a simple line drawing with a smattering of moon-runes. From there, I moved on to "A Part of the Shire" and, stepping up my game, the Map of Wilderland. I was then ready for the *pièce de résistance*.

For weeks, I spent hours at a time in my basement room, hunched over my antique oak worktable under a desk lamp with Queen playing over and over, painstakingly drawing every tree and hillcrest on Tolkien's legendary map.

The final toll in errors? One small drop of spilt ink somewhere in Eriador.

The project was a success. I learned a great deal of patience before I was fourteen, and those four maps hung on the walls of my various abodes over the years.

Finally, about fifteen years ago, I entrusted the maps to my four nephews, Jacob, Rick, Daniel, and Robert. I'm not sure if they still have them.

I was reminded of all of this because of a fabulous leather satchel that long-time friend and fellow Tolkien fan Brenda Dyrdahl ran across at the Puyallup fair, onto which the leather crafter had carved the Middle-earth map.

Sheesh! I never would have thought of *that*.

These days I apply my patience to other crafts… but wow.

What a nutty kid I was.

■

Michelle

I had the most remarkably comic conversation last night with my fiancée Misuk Ko, whom I have been slowly and wonderfully getting to know over the months I have been in the Methow valley—and it all started with something I wrote several years ago.

"So I've always meant to ask you. Who was this Michelle that you were in love with?" Misuk asked.

Right off the bat, I was truly stumped. Where, I inquired, had the idea come from that I'd ever been in love with a woman named Michelle?

"You wrote about her on your blog."

Baffled again. I've only known two Michelles in my adult life well enough to have possibly written about them... and while I was probably smitten with both of them at some point, I wouldn't say that I had been "in love" with either.

And if I had been, I most definitely would not have written about it. (I did pretend to be Michelle Tuck's boyfriend at Redwood Theater cast parties from time to time... but playing a doctor on TV, as they say, does not make one so.)

"Yes," Misuk insisted. "I read on your blog about a woman named Michelle. It was when you were in college."

Oh. Well, the only Michelle I knew in college was Michelle Noland, the Springsteen fan and keyboard player for the band in which I played sax. But again... wow. What would I have written on my blog about the "pee-na-ner" player? Other than her joking about the strange way in which she grew up saying "piano"? I've mentioned Ms. Noland in passing in the Wonderstruck notes, but not, as far as I knew, in my blog.

"You were doing theater and going to Bible college."

Bible college. And theater. Now, that would definitely have had to be Michelle Tuck.

But, wow. What did I ever write about Michelle Tuck? And in a fashion that would have conveyed I was in love with her?

"And you would meet her in the cafeteria. She was serving meals."

Whaaa-aaaat?

At this point, I felt like I was stepping into an episode of *The Twilight Zone*. Now, I suppose I could have just shrugged my shoulders or chalked things up to Misuk's tenuous but tenacious grasp of the English language, as one might expect of a native speaker of Korean.

But by this time I was truly intrigued. I paused the conversation long enough to Google my own blog.

As I suspected, I didn't come up with a lot of hits. In fact, there were exactly two. The first was a decidedly brief mention of Michelle Noland in an essay I wrote about the passing of saxman Clarence Clemons.

The second was… Michelle Pfeiffer.

This is what I had written:

> I was once again enrolled in college, matriculated at a lush East Coast brick-and-ivy league school. Instead of living in a dorm, I lived in a country boarding house on an actual working farm and ate meals at the table with Farmer John himself. His lovely daughter served the meals.
>
> The walk to school was leisurely and equally lovely, down country lanes lined with stately trees glowing in the morning light. Pastures segregated by stone walls undulated over the hills. Goats and cattle quietly grazed.
>
> The campus itself was on the outskirts of a small, sleepy, provincial town—somewhere near Gettysburg. The student body numbered in the mere hundreds, and my fellow classmates were all industrious and relentlessly pleasant. Learning was a joy for all.
>
> At the end of my idyllic days, I returned languidly home at the golden hour down the same country lanes. The scene was so bucolic that goats floated over the pastures, bleating contentedly.
>
> Yes, you read that right. The goats floated over the pastures.
>
> And then I would return to the Pfeiffer boarding house for a sumptuous home-cooked dinner served by the farmer's daughter.
>
> Named Michelle.

Yes, *that* Michelle.

Did I mention this was an exceedingly pleasant dream?

I had to laugh heartily. Michelle Pfeiffer. Oh, yes.

But Misuk had missed that part about "exceedingly pleasant dream."

Too funny.

■

Bos

Was it just a decade ago that I first encountered Monique Bos?

Why, it must have been, though that seems hard to believe. Some people feel like they've been your friends forever.

For reasons long forgotten, Monique and I entered into a correspondence over the copious writing (of many, many scribes) that Jenn and I were editing and publishing at the website *Hollywood Jesus*. It was not a "Christian" publication aimed at preaching to the choir; rather, it was geared toward those who at one point or another grew disillusioned (or became damaged) by the flaccidity or hypocrisies of the Church, or who were so skeptical of religion that their curiosity about Jesus couldn't be satisfied in conventional ways. HJ was not "open-minded" so much as "free-form." It didn't really matter what point of view you came from, as long as the ideas of Jesus intrigued you in some way.

> About a month ago, I heard a quote that socked me hard and has stayed with me: "What punishments of God are not gifts?" (From what I can determine, it's Stephen Colbert paraphrasing Tolkien.)
>
> Seven powerful words that made perfect, albeit painful, sense of my summer, and more broadly the trajectory my life has been on for the past few years.

> To me, this doesn't mean all punishments are gifts, but it serves as an attitude check when I feel like I'm being punished, a reminder that some of the most painful experiences in my life have led to the greatest growth. That at least some of the time, the seasons of suffering and anguish and challenge do carry a redemptive purpose.

Monique is a writer, and she published these words on Facebook last week.

During my early correspondence with Monique I was impressed enough with her intelligence, fluency, and coherence that I recruited her to write an internal critique column at *Hollywood Jesus*—a sort of built-in B.S. meter that would hold our writers' feet to the Holy Fire and call us to account when we were being fatuous or Pharisaical.

> The next day, I went to Mass with a friend. The priest talked about forest fires as a metaphor for the tough work God does in our lives: fire not as a destructive force but as a means to purify us, clean out the deadwood, and make room for new growth. His message, especially on the heels of the Colbert quote, reminded me of my favorite Stephen King novel, *Desperation*, which follows a similar theme: The love of God is cruel, and the cruelty of God is a refining fire. This is a brutally hard concept, but I can trace its truth throughout my life in ways I couldn't even a few months ago.

The proposed HJ column never got off the ground, mostly because I was on the way out the door at the time. But just about the time Monique moved to Lynnwood, Washington, only a forty-minute drive distant—a drive that I would never make—I discovered her novel *The Dark Jests of Lost Ghosts*.

When I pulled up stakes and moved to Twisp a year ago, I (heretically) divested myself of nearly every non-Tarkington book I owned, including all my Tolkiens, Lewises, and Charlie Russells.

What did I keep? Just Norman Dubie, Wilfred Owen, and... *Dark Jests*. The book is that good.

> I wish I could say all these profound quotes and epiphanies have brought me to a place of peace and wisdom. Actually, I'm impatient and frustrated. I'm ready for the damn fire to be out, but every time I think it's finished burning, a spark catches somewhere and I'm back to squinting through the smoke. Some of the losses continue to fester. I've had to walk away from people and things that have left jagged holes. In other situations, I'm struggling with whether and when and how to move on. I want to step fully into the season of new growth, and I don't know whether I'm holding myself back or still have necessary lessons to learn before the final embers are quenched.

Monique's 2010 novel is set in Savannah, Georgia, a city she knows quite well (and lives close to now). But the story she tells is neither quaint nor Southern Gothically romanticized; no, that would be too easy.

If *Midnight in the Garden of Good and Evil* is the most famous face of Savannah, *The Dark Jests of Lost Ghosts* might well be subtitled "Long After Midnight in the Abandoned Bowels of the Devil's Rootcellar."

Monique is a writer of horror, and like the best writers of horror she takes the power and reality of evil in our world terribly seriously. Her words do not entertain; they grip, and they squeeze. Her choice to publicize her latest story, "Matriarchy," with an image of Ligeia, her pet python, couldn't be more appropriate.

Dark Jests is told through the first-person present-tensed voices of myriad characters—victims, children and teens, a journalist, traumatized family members. Monique captures each of these voices in a unique and telling fashion as the story of a haunted house—a piece of the very Earth, a neighborhood, a borough, a city, and nation—possessed by the simple and deeply profound evils that we all embrace slithers out.

Sylvia Vale: "There is evil at 616 Yamasee for which I have no cure, wrongness that goes so deep and stretches so far back that no one can assuage it."

Maggie Carter: "Whatever was torturing her was too ancient and strong and evil for us or even for a minister who didn't but half believe in it."

Savannah: "smells foul. The stench from the paper mill stains the air: putrid-sweet, heavy, hijacking the miasmic swamp currents. Presses against sinuses and noses and mouths, seeps into buildings… The guidebooks didn't warn you, did they?"

Jester: "Turn your gazes from me, your gracious faces, your vicious visages. Deafen your ears to my chattering, my nattering, for what do I matter? What matter am I? I flatter myself. I shatter into crystal pieces of soul, unwhole, unholy."

The novel, like any hard truth, is not pleasant and is likely too dark for many readers. But darkness is a very real place, and those who come from pitched blackness into real light have an appreciation for it that others cannot fathom. And perhaps a sense of guilt for having been delivered, for not being able to drag along the other lost ghosts, for those they "failed to save."

> But God can only deliver one of us at a time, because in the moment of crisis there is only ever He and Ye. All else fades. All that to say, please be patient with me. And understand that suffering—and the quest to make sense of it, should we believe that's even possible and desire to do so—is very personal and individual. We can't tell other people why they're going through whatever challenges they're facing, and we can't give them a timeline for moving on/past/through, and we can't expect their paths to look the same as ours. I'm just sharing these thoughts tonight because they're important to me, and I hope they will be meaningful to someone else.

What a boon this friend has been to me through years of pain, and a season of renewal.

■

Four Loves

I have been particularly preoccupied of late with being astounded by four loves: first, a love about which I have not yet found the words to write; second, the storied love of Sheldon Vanauken for his wife, Jean; third, the more famous love of Vanauken's friend C.S. Lewis for his wife, Joy; and finally my own grand love for my late wife, Jenn, who passed away on this day two years ago.

I have been preoccupied because these loves are all strikingly connected.

Twice this year I have read Vanauken's *A Severe Mercy*, which I stumbled upon at a thrift store. The book, which includes correspondence with Vanauken's spiritual mentor Lewis (known as "Jack" to friends), tells of his idealistic romance with and subsequent marriage to Jean Davis (or "Davy"), her near-death bout with liver failure, her recovery and subsequent relapse, her passing at a mere forty-one years of age, Vanauken's grief, and the cessation of his mourning.

My first time through the book, the urge to write a Wonderstruck column arose a dozen times at least; but I felt doing so would somehow interrupt and dishonor the sanctity of the experience of absorbing such a stirring and insightful memoir. The fact that the narrative increasingly mirrored my own experience of Jenn's love and death, and of my mourning, confirmed my instinct. I did not dog-ear or highlight a single page, instead taking it all keenly to heart rather than engaging Vanauken with my brain-pan.

A couple of months ago, I was drawn a second time to the book, and this time I took a highlighter to it with a vengeance. I dwelt with it in chunks, intending to share as many wonderstruck words as I could find. But I have still not found that I can do so. I have intended to write so much but have not been able.

If you know me, you know that the issue is not that I am blocked; no, words have continued to pour out of me. But there are simply far, far too many things that I would like to say about Vanauken's book.

What I can tell you is this. I do not believe that the universe intends all men to love a woman in the way that I loved Jenn, the way that Sheldon loved Davy, and the way that Jack loved Joy… for two reasons.

First, empirical data bears it out. Only a privileged, tragic few husbands come to the point of their wife's terribly premature death with the flush of idealistic romantic love still untarnished; serve as caregiver and companion through a prolonged and mysterious illness; watch as their lover passes in great grace and closeness to Christ; and then contemplate a long future in the face of the void left behind. Were this the design of things, the pattern would be borne out with far more regularity than it is.

Second, theory and theology, history and practice, all bear out my belief that God has unique lessons for us all; or rather, that we each have specific needs that can only be satisfied in custom-designed ways. That Jack, Sheldon, and I all shared a common need that could only be met via a strikingly similar and monumental pain and sorrow is remarkable; but this cannot and should not be thought of as normative.

The path which I have walked would break many a man or woman; and the crosses which others have borne would certainly have crushed me.

The last thing I would want is for anyone to feel as if they had "missed out" on something because of comparison to my story. It is simply true that we are not all designed to bear the same kind of burdens.

Similarly, the universe does not dispense love in a cookie-cutter fashion. And I would, in all seriousness, not wish my experience upon my worst enemy, as bittersweet as it has been.

So what, precisely, was this need that Jack, Sheldon, and I shared? I will speak in the first person, for me rather than for us, in answering the question—although Sheldon certainly said the same for himself in his book, as Lewis also did less directly in *A Grief Observed*.

What I needed was to discover the jealousy that I held in my heart toward God—that I begrudged Jenn the closeness she developed for her Savior; that, as the suffering drew on, her love for Him became greater and more urgent than her love for me; that the energy she put into loving others because of that great love for Him left less energy for loving me; that Jenn could see this jealousy and that her final great concern for me was not that I would love her any less, just as she had not loved me any less, but that I would simply learn to love

God more. And that I could not learn this kind of love for Christ as long as Jenn continued to suffer, because as the suffering increased so also increased my devotion to my earthly love through the demand for ever-more selflessness in her service.

Only through Jenn's death—the beauty and peace of that death, and my acceptance of that death—could I learn this other love and stop being jealous of what was God's all along to give and Jenn's to freely reciprocate.

And it was God's great kindness to honor Jenn's wish for me through a transcendent beauty in her and the preservation of the love we shared.

All loves must die, wrote Lewis; but they do not all die in the same way. Jenn and I were blessed to have ours endure as long as her body survived. This is what Lewis and Vanauken, as writers, came to call "the severe mercy."

The preservation of idyllic romantic love to the point of death is a grand ideal indeed, and a tremendously merciful gift when it can be held; but parting with it at the point of death is most, most severe—a wound from which one does not ever recover. One may get past it, yes, in much the same way that one may learn to live without a leg or an arm; but the loss is still keenly felt.

In fact, the more one recovers, the more keenly the loss may be felt. As Lewis wrote, "One must have the capacity for happiness in order to be fully aware of its absence."

So, two years down the road, my capacity for happiness has increased greatly. For that I am grateful. I have been continuously wonderstruck by what the universe holds and impressed at humanity's appetite and desire for wonder. I have found that love did not die with Jenn, but that it continues to grow and flourish in the world around me.

But the tears still flow, when the time is right. Such as when I read yesterday, in the epilogue of *A Severe Mercy*, of Sheldon's dream of Davy on the eve of the second anniversary of her death; as I recalled Lewis's own death on November 22, the same date of Jenn's passing two years ago; as I read Sheldon's words of self-incrimination—his musing that Davy's death was necessary because of his own hardness of heart, that somehow he was to blame for Davy's illness. That resonated with me.

What if I had learnt of my jealousy in some other way than through Jenn's death? Would her suffering have been necessary? If she had lived, would our love have died a more natural, pedestrian, and ignoble death?

Sheldon agonizes through these and many other questions, and I wept through them all, once again.

Oh, Sheldon. I believe you ultimately learned, though you did not write of it, that all things are as they must be—and as they ever were, and ever will be.

We cannot play at what-ifs. As you wrote, we are harried by time; as Lewis suggested, we were not made for time, but for eternity; time is but one measure of the magnitude of wonder.

Do not begrudge that measure, as limited and paltry as it is; for the metaphor, at the very least, allows us to say, "This is when my love began," and that is sweet.

And, in a positive negativity, it allows us to glimpse what "without end" may possibly signify. Davy, I can assure you, sees, has seen, and will always see that her love for you has been perfected, Van. But then, you see that now, too. As does Joy, and as does Jack. And as does Jenn.

There are no "what-ifs" whatsoever; and yet there are an infinite number, all satisfied in a single "then."

Goodbye, then, Sheldon. Thank you.

Thank you for *A Severe Mercy*.

Wonderstruck.

■

A Dream of Robin and Frog

I stood on a stretch of asphalt in an evergreen forest.

From my vantage point, I could see the highway winding off for several miles, down and away from where I stood. At the nearest switchback of the looping roadway, the treetops were near eye-level.

I had recently completed an extraordinary cross-continental trek on foot with a group of trusted friends—a group that included my former engineering chum Jon Kottwitz, an American (red) robin, and an ordinary (if large) swamp frog.

To say that the robin and the frog—whose name was Tommy—had bonded during that overland ordeal would be an understatement. They were inseparable.

It had been rather comical, day after day, watching the robin flit from branch to branch while Tommy leapt along, several feet below the branches but always keeping pace.

To be fair, the robin had paced itself so that Tommy could keep up; but eventually, Tommy had upped his game and learned not only to hop more vigorously, but had also turned Tarzan—learning to use his forelegs like a tree-frog does, swinging from branchlet to branchlet and leveraging his prodigious hind legs in concert with grasps and lunges.

To onlookers, we two humans and our avian and amphibious friends must have seemed a bit of a tall tale in the flesh. But we had completed our travels in harmony and good spirits. We fit well together.

So it was with some chagrin that I watched what now transpired.

The robin had decided that he (or was it a he? I was not really sure how to distinguish the sex of birds, aside from coloring) was long overdue at home back east and was now winging it back down that forest road.

But pacing to accommodate Tommy had gone out the window. He was flying the way a robin normally does, not chattering from branch to branch but "as the crow flies."

Tommy had not caught on to the robin's plans, so from where I stood I could see him launching himself from treetop to treetop in hot pursuit—doing well to move as quickly as he was. You know, swamp frogs don't ordinarily travel quickly in the crowns of trees.

But Tommy was nonetheless losing ground badly. I called out to the robin, "You're going too fast! There's no way Tommy can keep up! You'll kill him!" But it was no use. The robin had determined to leave, and there was no dissuading him.

I needed to stop Tommy. So I either jumped in my car or ran down the tarmac—my dream was very unclear on this point—and my search confirmed my worst fear: The pace of the chase had indeed undone Tommy, and he had fallen into the roadway... where he had been run over by a passing car.

Lying there on his back, his belly as white as the underside of a pre-teen's forearm, Tommy's right limbs had been entirely shorn away, presumably mashed into the treads of some steel radial now miles away.

I collected what was left of Tommy's panting body and returned to where Jon stood waiting. He had been joined by a stranger.

"That doesn't look good," Jon said as I laid Tommy out on the needled gravel hardpack of the road's shoulder. As we watched, bodily fluids that looked like uncooked scrambled egg oozed from the places where his legs had recently been.

"You know," said the stranger, "I've heard that some frogs can regrow body parts that they've lost." He was a biologist and had some learning in this area.

"I was gonna say…" I trailed off. "Cuz look: that eggy stuff is already turning into legs.

"This is all because of the long trip we've just completed," I began to explain. And I told of the bond that Tommy and the robin had developed.

"So Tommy just couldn't help but chase after the robin when he left. They had grown so close over the—" And I turned to Jon here for help. "—what? three months or so that it took us to hike from Maine to Washington."

"A week," Jon deadpanned.

"Right, a week." I stood corrected. It had just seemed like months, I guess.

Jon was always better with numbers.

■

Experiencing God

March 12, 9:00 PM, Winthrop, Washington.

Toward the end of the second night of a new study titled *Experiencing God*, the workbook asked me to write down the statement or Scripture that most stuck with me from the day's assignment.

Before I go further, I will remark that Henry Blackaby's *Experiencing God* has been in my possession for somewhere around a year. Following a long talk with Dale and Sue Peterson at Winthrop Friendship Alliance Church, I had borrowed a copy from the church library with their encouragement. It certainly sounded like good material and had also come with recommendations from other people with whom Sue had recently gone through the material.

Now, I don't tend to pick up books and just start reading them. I sit with them a while, put them on the shelf, and ask, "Does this feel like the right time for me to read this? Yes, I know other people love this… but is the universe begging me to dive into this right now?" And if the answer is not a solid yes, I will just let the book rest.

In the twelve or so months since I picked up this workbook, I have become as thick as thieves with the little knot of couples that Sue leads through various studies. As a follow-on to our prolonged course through *How We Love*, the ladies in the group decided that it would be a good time to revisit *Experiencing God*. Without me even really thinking about it, the universe declared *Now is the time*, and I simply went along for the ride.

Three of the eight of us couldn't make it for all of our initial meeting Tuesday night, but we went right on ahead as planned anyway, expecting to catch the others up as we went. That meant plowing right into the near-daily assignments in prep for the next of our weekly meetings.

This wouldn't have been possible just a couple of weeks ago, as my life routines have been completely upended over the last three months. But this week, the time was absolutely right to be able to start into a regular routine of study. Hunkering down due to Covid-19 evening event cancellations certainly hasn't hurt.

So Thursday night at 9 PM I'm winding down my daily study and I get that instruction to write down the statement or Scripture that stood out to me. Without hesitating, I wrote:

"What is God doing?"

As the last few characters bled out of my pen, a little rush of adrenaline went through me.

"Oh my. I've written that down before! "And I think I know when.

"No… It couldn't be. That would just be too much of a coincidence."

I rose to retrieve the journal which holds the notes and poetry fragments that I've been jotting down for three years.

I flipped through the pages until I saw the words I was looking for. There at the very bottom of the sheet, in a large scrawl, was: *"God, what are you doing?"*

They were words I had yelled at the top of my lungs just prior to scribbling them down.

The date at the top of the page: March 12, 2018.

Two years prior, to the day.

It was the day I discovered *Wonderstruck*.

I did not begin writing the Wonderstruck column until some weeks later, after Jenn's Celebration of Life service; but March 12, 2018, was the day that serendipity really started doing its work on me: the day that God really grabbed me and said, "I want you to be amazed at what I am doing… not that I want you to understand it all, but I do want you to always be aware that I am working. Every day. Be encouraged, even when you feel like you are in the dark."

And boy, was I really in the dark that day. I had come completely unmoored over the weekend and had been hammered by some realizations about myself that were terribly unsettling. And yet it was a weekend that was saturated with a tidal wave of highly improbably coincidences.

By the time the afternoon of Monday, March 12, had rolled around, the momentum of it all was like the waves that crash on that crazy lighthouse in La Jumet, France. The mind boggling continued well into the evening, and quite honestly my life has never been the same since.

That evening, I wrote: "I heard from God today in a most extraordinary way, a very profound and direct way that I have not experienced in twenty years—words of great encouragement and hope which affirm that you have done, and are doing, the right things. Do not doubt yourself. You have not made mistakes. Everything—*every* thing—has led to where you are today, right now. Everything."

My life took a turn that day; four months later, another wild weekend of serendipity sent me to the Methow… and into a group study with Dale and Sue Peterson.

And *Experiencing God*.

And a particular assignment on the evening of March 12, 2020.

How also serendipitous that two years later, to the very day, the words that I wrote down from a time-is-just-right assignment would lead me back to the very note that started it all.

Wonderstruck.

■

March 11, 2018

Sunday. My sister Elane and I were the first to arrive at Claim Jumper for her birthday, and we had a good chance to talk.

After hearing about my disappointing breakup of the previous morning—and about which I have written earlier in connection to that wedding rehearsal dream—Elane said, "To be perfectly honest, Greg—for women my age, you are the ideal man we are all hoping to find. But for independent women like me, you would be overwhelming." She used that particular word without me having mentioned that my ex had also used it. I would journal later that day, "So I guess God needs to send me to a woman I either will not overwhelm or who *wants* to be overwhelmed!"

Other family members began to arrive—and at this point I could start cataloguing for you the things which followed as very curious coincidences… but I would start repeating myself, and frequently. So I will skip the commentary and just relate the facts.

My sister-in-law, Sally, who lives in Puyallup, bought *exactly the same birthday card* for Elane that I had purchased a hundred miles away the day before, and Elane opened Sally's card immediately after mine. Elane raised an eyebrow in my direction at that, and she didn't know the half of it.

Next up was the card that Elane's son Jacob bought for her—*exactly the same card I had purchased for my ex* the previous day. At the same time and place I had purchased Elane's birthday card. No kidding. And it was *not* a birthday card, just a generic card that might happen to suit either a birthday or a breakup. Yeah. I leaned over to Elane and whispered some words. She looked back at me with one of her patented *you-must-be-kidding-me* looks.

A good deal of storytelling followed, given that it was Elane's 60th birthday celebration, and having rehearsed a family story of Queen's *A Night at the Opera* in the spa with my ex three nights prior, I shared it with the whole family, including Elane's kids and their significant others. Everyone, including Elane and my brother Bob, were totally engaged with the story. It involved Bob, because his then-girlfriend Linda Stanford had given me the album as an early Christmas gift. It involved Elane, because she and I were housesitting for one of her friends on a Sunday morning when we first listened to the album. And it involved both Mom and Dad, because they had listened to the album repeatedly at bedtime when they shared basement space with me while Grandma Wright was ensconced for several weeks in the master bedroom upstairs. They all completely affirmed how special that experience was and how it not only changed my life but the whole family's life for years afterward: how Elane would buy the new Queen albums and then share them with me; how we went to three Queen concerts together; how Bob was so impressed with the trust that Elane placed in me with her things; how Mom would sometimes ask me to play the second side of *A Night at the Opera* at bedtime because it helped her sleep.

I had never felt so warmly received and understood by my family, as an adult, as I did that Sunday afternoon. It was wonderful.

Later, my ex would write, "Be encouraged, Greg! God has His timing, He loves us, He has reasons for doing what He does! This is as much for me, as you!

"Just had a thought! I think if I had been at Elane's celebration, it would have really really changed what went on between you, your siblings, your mom, Queen... I am so grateful for God's wisdom of the timing of things. Wow! Double wow!"

To be honest, my initial desire to have her with me at Elane's birthday was something like saying to my family, "Look—I really don't *need* your understanding, which I don't feel I have ever had. I don't need it now because I've got this woman. She gets me, and she's wonderful. So what you all think *really doesn't matter*." I planned to use her as a shield from my family.

Yet because God had other ideas than my own petty plans, and because I was a different man that afternoon than I had been even a week prior—more humble, more surrendered to God—I was instead able to be with my family and say, "Look, here I am. *This is all I've got*. It's all I will ever have to offer. I love you, and I need your love." And they gave it to me. And my life with them changed. Dramatically. Not that they noticed, probably. But that was a big, big deal nonetheless.

Thanks to a romantic rejection.

■

Marriage

March 23, 2020, Winthrop, Washington.

5:00 AM. My alarm wakes me up, as usual on a Monday.

Now, ordinarily I am awake by 5:00 or 5:30, without any need for an alarm. (Several years of living with my former cat Bearette trained me well.) But on most "work days," I set my alarm anyway, just as a matter of discipline.

I am particularly disciplined on Mondays, because I have a standing one-hour online prayer meeting at 6 AM with the international team producing *Let Me Have My Son* for Messenger Films.

I never sleep through my alarm and hardly ever drift back to sleep after turning the alarm off.

5:05 AM. I am blissfully back in dreamland. Go figure.

6:00 AM. I am startled awake by an alarm I don't recognize. And it's in a different room. Somewhere.

I stumble out of bed and go in search of the offending noise. I locate it in the guest room.

The alarm is blaring from a clock I had just plugged in the previous evening. Prior to that, there had been no alarm in the guest room. Prior to that, this alarm clock had only been used in the bathroom in the house where I used to live… and as you can imagine, there is rarely an occasion to have an alarm set in a bathroom.

Why was the alarm set for 6:00 AM? I have no idea. It would have been set that way at least two years ago.

Why was the alarm even on? I have no idea.

How did the battery backup last all that time? I have no idea.

Who set the alarm for 6:00 AM? Most likely Jenn, I guess, even though she never rose to an alarm. It was her clock, her bathroom timepiece.

Why did I notice that the alarm was an hour off when I plugged it in, and why did I set it for the correct time? Because I can't stand to have clocks with the wrong time.

Why did I oversleep my alarm? And why has the guest room alarm happened to wake me on time for my weekly Messenger Films call?

Well, I can tell you that I sure have my radar up while we talk and pray. I am sure that the universe really wants me on that call today. Something special is sure to be discussed!

Well, Cheryl, director Cris Krusen's wife, is on the call. That is unusual. And she talks about the burden God had placed on her heart for prayer and fasting this year... well before anyone had heard about Covid-19.

And Cristóbal tells an amazing story about how peace came to the recent shoot in Mexico in the form of Edgar Shalom Nava, who ended up cast at the eleventh hour in the role of David.

Brian talks about the impact of Covid-19 in Berlin, while Greg Silker speaks about his dream of establishing an indie Skywalker Ranch-type facility in the Minneapolis area. We pray through concerns relayed by Daniel Leafblad and Loyd Jenkins via email.

But by the time I leave the call, I feel like I must have missed something. Yes, those are all special stories and prayers… but nothing jumps out as *the* thing for which I have been extraordinarily roused at 6:00 AM.

I am not wonderstruck by the call. (Sorry, crew.)

From there, my morning proceeds as usual. I shall spare you the details. You probably don't want to know how I shower, dress, or brush my teeth. Never mind deodorant or other personal hygiene routines.

I keep my radar open. The strangeness of that 6:00 AM alarm tells me that I will be wonderstruck by something today.

■

March 23, 1:00 PM.

After lunch, I am packing up some boxes when I run across a note from Jenn tucked in the bottom of a drawer. It reads:

> Hello, my love! Just had to wish you a good day! I love you! I know you miss me as much as I miss you—maybe even more. But I couldn't let a day go by without declaring my absolute love for you. It hurts so bad to be apart, but God is with us and nothing can divide the three of us. Let distance be but a breath away. Let us sleep soundly and look anxiously, anticipating our reunion. I love you!

March 24, 1998, was the day that Jenn and I joined ourselves for eternity. Twenty-two years ago. We later married on August 22, 1999.

■

March 24, 2020. 4:34 PM.

I have married again, this time Misuk Ko.

Misuk chose this date for our wedding because it is her birthday, and because she knew—from the first time she read my blog—that March 24 was a very special date for Jenn and me.

Misuk is a very special woman.

Jenn will be a part of this marriage, and so will Misuk's late husband, Shawn Johnston.

Yes, Jenn. Let distance be but a breath away. Let us all sleep soundly in this peace. What a grand reunion the four of us—no, the five of us—shall have. Nothing shall divide us!

Wonderstruck.

■

Civil Discourse

I would like to be able to say that I am amazed at the wonderful, balanced, thoughtful dialogue taking place on social media in these turbulent times.

Alas, it is not only obvious that public discourse has taken a nose dive in general; but even my favorite dialogicians have gone relatively silent. In some cases, thoughtsmiths have simply chosen to avoid the general toxicity for a time; in some cases, public comment has been so trollish that comments have been shut down and dialogue turned into monologue; while in others, it seems that regular commenters have simply vanished, perhaps because they have tired of the overt war that conversation has become… or because they have grown exhausted with constant reminders that we are all capable of much better behavior.

Surprisingly, perhaps, though, I have found some remarkable examples of civil discourse in… wait for it… Scripture.

Yes, in one of the most incendiary contexts and explosive periods of history—the height of the Roman Empire's dominance, rife with racial oppression, brutal tyranny, explicit religious persecution, corrupt and merciless law enforcement, outright disregard for personal rights, violent protests and counterprotests, assassinations, and attempts at insurrection—Jesus and his Apostles found themselves having very different public conversations than those around them.

Some examples: "Love your enemies, and pray for those who persecute you."

"If your enemy strikes you, turn the other cheek."

"As far as it depends on you, be at peace with everyone."

"Render unto Caesar what is Caesar's, and unto God what is God's."

"They will know you are my disciples by your love."

"Make the Master proud of you by being good citizens."

"It is God's will that by doing good you might cure the ignorance of fools who think you're a danger to society."

"Exercise your freedom by serving God, not by breaking the rules."

Even at the point of death, both Jesus and Stephen were praying for mercy on their state-sanctioned murderers.

Now, if you are not one who follows Christ, you can discount all of this outright as either fanciful or unrealistic, and with no quibbles from me. But if you claim to follow Christ, these are words *you have to deal with*.

They were uttered not by men who merely had their civil rights infringed, or who were concerned about some eventual takeover by a nebulous world conspiracy. These were the words of men who actually suffered horribly, and died terrible deaths, at the hands of those who could not abide their message.

And what was their message?

Not one of rebellion or resistance, but one of God's mercy and love, even for the rebellious.

Yet today, so many followers of Christ, on both sides of the political aisle, from the safety of their own homes and keyboards, have abandoned the witness and example of their Master in favor of the "mic drop" and the desire to verbally destroy their enemies—and not in the interest of promoting the love of God through Christ, but often in the interest of promoting the words and ideas of complete strangers... or worse yet, their own self-interest, the status quo, throwing out the baby with the bath water, or some fanciful past to which we simply cannot return.

Social justice and liberty are indeed noble pursuits; both are decidedly worth defending. But are we all speaking as well in defense of our causes as we might? And have we chosen the right causes? The testimony of Scripture, as it always should, suggests that we are not, and have not.

It is possible to be both a good citizen and passionately and righteously countercultural; and the path to that end, for the believer, always runs through the filter called the Gospel.

The recipe? In humility, remember for whom you speak: not yourself, as a believer, but for Christ. And do so "full of the Spirit," rather than full of a load of something very, very else.

Wanna be wonderstruck? Take some time this week to read through the Acts of the Apostles. You will be shocked at how often the phrase "full of the Spirit" crops up, and at how different your witness to this culture might be... with a little help from your Friend and Advocate.

> Love is very patient and kind, never jealous or envious, never boastful or proud, never haughty or selfish or rude. Love does not demand its own way. It is not irritable or touchy. It does not hold grudges and will hardly even notice when others do it wrong. It is never glad about injustice, but rejoices whenever truth wins out. If you love someone, you will be loyal to him no matter what the cost. You will always believe in him, always expect the best of him, and always stand your ground in defending him. (I Cor. 13:4-7, *The Living Bible*)

I am disappointed in a lot of what I see right now. But I am not pessimistic. Growing pains are always followed by great things.

And the Spirit is here.

And God is about to do amazing things that we would not believe if we were told. He *always* is.

Believe it?

■

Allegiance

Today, I shall put on my pastor hat.

Actually, I'm *always* wearing my pastor hat, but you may not realize it. That's because being a pastor very often—most often, perhaps?—looks very ordinary, just as a shepherd taking a flock out to pasture looks very ordinary.

Every once in a while, though, a pastor must look and feel like a pastor, as it were. That is, look and feel like the images we associate with pastors/ministers/priests/preachers. You know, all hellfire-and-brimstoney, lecturing, upbraiding, posturing. Up on the high horse. More like a prophet than a shepherd.

Did you know that most real pastors don't like that part of the job? They really prefer the walking alongside, the eating and the drinking, the lying down together in cool pastures. If you meet a pastor who really digs whipping the flock into a lather, you're probably dealing with a drill instructor or megalomaniac.

Or, perhaps, an honest-to-God prophet.

Pastors have, after all, ideally set themselves aside for ministry, declared themselves for God—put away their personal preferences for the sake of the Gospel—and sometimes (yea, verily, probably not often enough) have some uncomfortable words of truth to share.

So let me talk to you about *allegiance.*

I started reading Francis Chan's *Multiply* lately, as God has put the topic of discipleship on my heart this fall. The church I attend has also undertaken to examine the topic and will be using Chan's book as a guide.

It's a good choice, because Chan doesn't say, "I've got a proven plan for cranking out functional disciples of Christ, and here it is…" Instead he says, "There is no plan, really, aside from surrender to God. And this is what surrender looks like…"

And theologically speaking—according to the witness of Scripture—Chan is absolutely correct. "Stop whatever you are doing," says Jesus of Nazareth, "and follow me. See what I am doing, and do likewise.

"Further," says this Jesus, "you will be able to see what I am doing, after I am gone, by watching what my pastors are doing. And you can tell who they are because they imitate the Good Shepherd. *Don't fall for fakes.*"

This is an important point.

Who are your shepherds right now? Who are you following? Do they imitate the Good Shepherd? Or are they dancing to a different tune in this season of turmoil?

Who, or what, has your allegiance? Whom has your pastor apparently sworn to follow?

Says Chan of baptism, "When first-century Christians took this step of identifying themselves with the death and resurrection of Jesus, they were publicly declaring their allegiance to Christ."

Allegiance to Christ.

Have you taken the pledge?

Have you copied and pasted to Facebook or Signal?

Have you sworn, following the words of Jesus, that you refuse to serve any other master? That your allegiances aren't divided?

Is YHWH figuratively emblazoned across your forehead, or is something else scrawled there?

For here is sound teaching: You cannot serve both God and something else. Membership in the Kingdom of Heaven doesn't provide dual citizenship. You are either all in, or all out. You cannot follow the banner of heaven *and* your nation's flag. "Would that you were hot or cold," says Jesus to Laodicea. He's not a fan of lukewarm.

You may, following God's lead, *minister* to your nation—and I would certainly hope you do. But be perfectly clear about this: Your nation, no matter its boundaries or its administration, is continually and proactively engaged in obscenely immoral acts. The level of obscenity fluctuates at any given moment: Sometimes it looks more like assassination than genocide; sometimes it takes more of the flavor of a Pharisee walking by a mugged neighbor in a ditch than outright empire-building; sometimes it looks more like state-sanctioned advertising doublespeak than criminally self-serving "spin" of bald falsehood.

But make no mistake: Your nation's flag, whichever it be, *is not headed the same direction as Jesus.* "My kingdom is not of this world," he told Pilate. How much clearer do you need it?

You cannot take even three steps east of Eden and still be following your compass true north.

"The implications of this are huge," Chan continues regarding his words on allegiance. "Don't think of this as a merely theological issue." Pledging allegiance to Christ, and Christ alone, is the core issue for anyone who claims the name of Christ—who aspires to the appellation of *Christian*, or "little Christ," who desires to take the name of Christ but not in vain, whose aim is not just to "self-identify" with Jesus but actually live as He did.

"Jesus' commands do not come with exception clauses," says Chan, quite rightly. "He doesn't tell us to follow *unless* we're busy. He doesn't call us to love our neighbors"—or our enemies—"*unless* we don't feel prepared."

Is it feeling like I've got my pastor hat on yet? If you haven't blown me off by this point and are still reading but are fuming and angry, rest assured—I get it. I've been there. I completely understand the equivocation, the ambivalence, the *wait-this-is-treason* nausea in the gut.

But we all know how important the nation of Israel was (and is) to God, right? Can you imagine how the Apostles felt when they turned their back on that tradition to serve the Church Universal? When they stopped calling themselves Jews and started calling themselves Christians?

Or when they started dying, quite passively and without resistance, because their Christ and His Kingdom were more important than their nation? I'm sure they felt sick to their stomachs, too. Repenting—heading a different direction, turning aside toward the Kingdom of Heaven, which is *always* at hand—is never easy.

If turning away from national identity was right enough for the Apostles, it's certainly right enough for disciples today, too.

At no time in the church's history were its leaders more convinced of the imminent return of Christ than in the first century. At no time was the church more oppressed and under fire from the enemy. *And at no time was the church less concerned about earthly power and playing politics.* They saw themselves as ambassadors—emissaries of God's Kingdom, sent with a message to a dying world—even martyrs, if need be… but not participants. No. Get it?

So please don't think that any president or party is your savior or this nation's.

And please don't think that the real solution starts anywhere else than with *you*.

And *your allegiance*.

Choose this day who you will follow, to crib a line from the Old Testament's Joshua. 'Tis the season, after all.

And do be wonderstruck as you choose. Because *whatever* your hopes are for yourself, your family, your community, your nation, and this world…

God is able to do immeasurably *more* than you can ask or imagine.

That's the good news. Because whatever your vision for America, *you are wrong*. God has much more in store for America than such weak dreams. He has a vision for Kingdom, not Nation.

And he *does* want your allegiance.

You have pledged that at some point *to a flag*. We all have. So you know how to pledge allegiance.

Why not pledge it to the Creator of *all* flags?

∎

Democracy

From March 1995 through June 1997, I took night classes to complete a degree in ministry. At one point, as you might guess, I was required to take a course in Old Testament history.

Quite coincidentally—or perhaps not—about the same time I picked up a translation of Herodotus' *Histories*, which provides a fairly comprehensive digest of the events of the region that became the Greek Empire.

One of the stories that Herodotus relates is the overthrow of the Persian monarch by Darius the Great and his companions—who, in the wake of their insurrection, debate the best form of government to install.

And this is the part of the story that had me wonderstruck: One of the options they debated was... *a democracy*.

In a conversation that took place around 500 B.C.

Now, the education which I received taught me that democracy was really only first successfully implemented on a national scale in the United States, and that the first (ultimately failed) trial of the idea was in the city-state of Athens around 400 B.C. Even today *Wikipedia* states that "Athenian democracy is often described as the first known democracy in the world."

So... what were Darius and his pals doing discussing the merits and downfalls of democracy a hundred years prior to the "Athens experiment"?

And how did there come to be sufficient historic experience with democracies that Darius' crew could accurately assess its potential and pitfalls? That would mean democracies had to exist—to rise, be stable, and subsequently fall—multiple times, and hundreds of years prior to the Persian Empire... say, more than a thousand years before Christ.

What were these democracies? How is it that they had absolutely vanished from history, except as lessons learned for Darius and his revolutionaries?

Well, republics and democracies, like all governments, rise and fall. And when they fall, their falls can be so calamitous as to result in their complete annihilation. There are vast civilizations, such as that of the Scythians as one example, for whom there is but scant historical evidence.

But that is almost beside the point. Almost.

The second thing that struck me, even in 1996, was Darius' ability to accurately pinpoint the trajectory of our own democracy.

First, Megabyzus describes the problem of the governed in a democracy, which he considers "not the best advice. For there is nothing so void of understanding, nothing so full of wantonness, as the unwieldy rabble.

"It were folly not to be borne," he continues. "The tyrant, in all his doings, at least knows what is he about, but a mob is altogether devoid of knowledge; for how should there be any knowledge in a rabble, untaught, and with no natural sense of what is right and fit?

"It rushes wildly into state affairs with all the fury of a stream swollen in the winter, and confuses everything." Hm. Sounds vaguely reminiscent of the last twelve months of various protests.

Megabyzus concludes, "Let the enemies of the Persians be ruled by democracies; but let us choose out from the citizens a certain number of the worthiest, and put the government into their hands." Thus he argues for an oligarchy, a system of government which generally describes Russia or China today. These are words Vladimir Putin could have authored.

"All that Megabyzus said against democracy was well said," offers Darius, adding that "in a democracy, it is impossible but that there will be malpractices: these malpractices, however, do not lead to enmities, but to close friendships, which are formed among those engaged in them, who must hold well together to carry on their villainies."

Wow. Nailed it. Think of everyone who partied with Epstein. Not just the ones you don't like, but *everyone*.

"And so things go on," Darius asserts, "until a man stands forth as champion of the commonalty, and puts down the evil-doers. Straightway the author of so great a service is admired by all, and from being admired soon comes to be appointed king." This is precisely what January 6, "another day that will live in infamy," was all about. A well-founded mistrust of democratic malpractices, and of their perpetrators, and an understandable attempt to say, "No more!"

Republicans and Democrats alike have for decades fostered a false enmity, pretending to their constituents that the opposing side is the enemy when they know full well that a robust opposition is essential for the continued "balance" of power in a two-party system, a false biennial/quadrennial see-saw battle so ostensibly crucial that it prevents the rise of a meaningful third party. It has become inevitable that the governed would eventually lose trust in their system of governance and instead turn to some figurehead for salvation.

Any figurehead.

Darius and his buddies would not have been the least bit surprised by what transpired in Washington, D.C., yesterday. They might even have been there, participating in or leading an attempted coup. They would probably even have been successful.

What is truly surprising is that those who should know better—politicians who make a specialty of and a living from the study and implementation of politics—were apparently surprised and have for years been standing idly by or abetting while our democracy wandered down a very predictable path.

Well, it's not too late to learn from history. A strangely mild insurrection has been averted; but a rather more violent one is in the offing, I gather from the words of friends and acquaintances, if our elected officials don't straighten up and start governing for the people in unity for the greater good.

But we've got our own work cut out for us, too. We have far too great an appetite for bread and circuses. Our demagogues are of our own creation.

God help us all if we create a shadow puppet and then turn to that horrific creation for salvation. Actual democracy is a much better course.

And even then, God help us. The writing is probably on that wall, too.

■

Gifts

I was not one of those kids who got hyper-excited about Christmas morning... at least, not for the usual reasons.

I did look forward to getting together with extended family so that the cousins could engage in all sorts of unruly behavior that involved snowballs, pillows, and other mayhem-related imple-ments. When it was just our immediate family gathering on Christmas morning, though, I was actually less excited than I was on Saturday mornings. (No cartoons on TV.)

Part of this was due to the fact that opening Christmas gifts was usually a bit of a letdown. I should have been grateful, I know, because we always had gifts under the tree and because "hard times," such as they were, simply meant strange things in the larder (like halvah and chests full of frozen past-pull-date milk) rather than actual deprivation.

For Christmas, family protocol dictated that I put together a list of things I wanted, usually culled from the Sears and Montgomery Ward catalogs, with the expectation that Santa would deliver on one of the items listed. The problem: Usually there was just one thing I particularly wanted, and the rest of the items were filler.

But Santa didn't know that. Eight times out of ten what Santa delivered was filler.

And that was a problem because the other gifts I received at Christmas were like birthday presents in our family: practical stuff like shirts, socks, and maybe, in a good year, a new coat or boots. By and large, toys were acquired as somebody else's castoffs at the dump (or "transfer station," as it was called in civilized Seattle) or as hand-me-downs. (One caveat is that Bob, Elane, and I were pretty good, I think, at filling in with small gifts to one another. I still have, for instance, a Matchbox car transport truck that Elane gave me for my fifth birthday. Best gift ever!)

I did hit the jackpot two Christmases, however. One year it was the Daniel Boone flintlock rifle and pistol set. They used compression from caps to actually launch cork balls as projectiles from their steel muzzles. (Until very recently, I still had the pistol, too; I gave it to one of the Suter boys when I moved from Twisp to Winthrop when I married Misuk.)

The other item I really wanted another year was the Sears Western Town Set... and Santa delivered! Boy, howdy. I got at least a couple of good years from that set before I outgrew it... and it made its way, in various loads, to the, um, transfer station.

I am very glad, of course, that I not only outgrew the Sears Western Town but also my obsession with gifts and disappointment.

Here's a fact: The unexpected gifts we receive—which are myriad and glorious—far outstrip the gifts we expect... or the disappointment of not receiving what we expect. As the Apostle Paul writes, God desires more for us "than we could possibly ask or imagine"; and if we are patient, and have our eyes open, we eventually see that God always delivers.

Unexpected gifts in my life include two brilliant and wonderful marriages; countless priceless friends; so many sunrises, sunsets, mountain glades, and waterfalls… and, not least, the fact that I now help run a shop in a town that looks not too unlike that Sears catalog gift from decades ago.

How's that for delayed gratification, on a rather grand scale?

Yeah. Wonderstruck.

■

Unexpected Gifts

Weren't we just talking about unexpected gifts?

"Here's a fact," I wrote just two days ago. "The unexpected gifts we receive—which are myriad and glorious—far outstrip the gifts we expect… or the disappointment of not receiving what we expect."

And what to my wondering eyes should appear, less than twenty-four hours later, but a most unexpected gift!

Further, this was in fact the only packaged gift I received this Christmas. I am not complaining, mind you. I'll turn sixty next year, which means I've had a plenty long life to acquire stuff. For quite a long time now, my family has scuttled the usual patterns of gift-giving for birthdays and at Christmas. When the mood strikes us and we find something particular *a propos* and useful, we will send along a thoughtful little package… but not in the usual "Oh! I must find a gift for so-and-so!" sort of way. So, no… no packages under the Christmas tree for me. "All I need is the air that I breathe," as The Hollies sang decades ago.

So out of the blue comes this rather hefty box via USPS Priority Mail. It's from filmmaker and author Rick Stevenson, with whom I've been working on The 5000 Days Project and The Human Library Initiative for the last twelve years or so. Technically, he's a client of my consulting business… but calling him a client is a little insulting. Since I first met him over coffee at a Starbucks in Shoreline, Washington, with fellow media genius Paul Cranefield, Rick and I have seen eye to eye on the cinematic arts, independent artists, media distribution, the challenges and potential of youth in today's culture, what's worth paying attention to in politics, the nature of faith, and the importance of personal action in response to all of the above.

My work relationship with Rick, however, has nearly come to an end. I will continue to serve on the board of The Human Library Initiative… but my lately acquired roles as husband and retail proprietor have necessitated cutting back on my consulting, among other things. As a result, I am in the process of tapering off my work with The 5000 Days Project.

So the box I received from Rick was not really a Christmas present; it was sort of a severance package, if you will! And most unexpected.

I have to say, though, that it seemed to spring from my very thoughts. During dinner on Monday, I rather randomly mused about the nature of gift-giving and that the most meaningful gifts, if properly received, are gifts which are actually most meaningful to the giver. That is, something special shared of self. And the receiver takes it in as an act of empathy, of growing in knowledge of another human being.

I suppose the thought grew out of my role as a pastor and the nature of the Greatest Gift of the Christmas season. It was a theological thought. It was also a literary thought, metaphorical in nature.

Hold that thought.

What Rick gave me was an 1861 edition of Fleetwood's *Life of Christ*, from his personal collection. He acquired the tome, handsomely bound in metal-framed and -clasped leather boards, during his years in Oxford.

"I am pleased to gift you," Rick wrote in an accompanying letter, "with one of the most prized possessions from my book collection. Please accept this as a sign of thanks for the role you have played in my life. It's a wonderful book.

"And the main character? That Jesus guy? The best character yet."

Uh-huh.

Seriously. I think Rick and I would both agree that, in light of the Greatest Gift, all we truly need is the air that we breathe... "and to love you."

■

Work

I have always worked, as long as I can remember.

Okay, that's a little bit of an exaggeration. I did not start doing door-to-door direct sales of greeting cards, collectible postage stamps, and seed packets until I was seven years old... and I can, in fact, remember back further than that with a good deal of facility.

And I didn't have my first actual employer until I was ten years old and started delivering papers door-to-door, eventually migrating from my *Renton Record Chronicle* route to a *Seattle Times* route which I held until I was fifteen. Oh, those dark winter Sunday mornings! And only once was I ever quite sick enough to stay home and get Mom to cover for me. So by the time I was a teenager, I had already been both self-employed and worked on commission.

My first hourly-wage job came my way at just thirteen, a one-day-a-week gig as a church janitor. That led to my eighteen-month stint as a Beds Unlimited stock boy when I was a high school senior. (I first learned on this job the value of being hard-working and dependable. When the district manager was being difficult and told me, "I'm trying to run a store, Greg, and if you don't like it you can leave," and I left, the store manager called me at home and begged me to return. "I've already told Colin he can't be here any more when you're working.")

Admittedly, the scholarships I was on during my college years enabled me to get away with part-time jobs bussing tables, washing dishes, and trying to sort out microcomputer issues for the UW English department. (College summers were spent gloriously working for King County Parks at Seahurst on Puget Sound.) So "I have always worked" is also a bit of a stretch in that regard.

With marketable skills in computer science, though, I went straight from college into the salaried workforce at Boeing, finding safer ways to test-fire Peacekeeper missiles (!!), and after a short stint there I spent a dozen years in cardiac science at Quinton Instrument Company, earning a patent for the final project I managed there.

In 1997, I went into ministry (as a calling, not a job) and retired from engineering in 1998, having conceived of a way to work at a "semi-retired" level for the remainder of my days. By 2000 I had migrated into consulting both as an editor and as a techie... and while my cumulative workload over these last twenty years has ranged from ten to seventy hours per week, one characteristic of my days has remained the same.

Six to seven days a week, for the last twenty years, the first two to three hours after rising early have been devoted to paying attention to someone else's business. That of my clients, to be sure, but for far too long I have not had the luxury of waking up and thinking, "What would I like to do this morning? Or should I just go back to sleep?"

Well, after a very long slog, that has changed this week. And oh, how different it feels!

I am still very fully and gainfully occupied running The Iron Horse in Winthrop with my wife Misuk… but I have wrapped up my consulting work and some volunteer work with the boards of local nonprofits. To start the day reading, writing, thinking, praying… what a joy!

I would like to say that my long work history has been the beneficiary of some ethic instilled by my father, a Boeing lifer; but I have to say that neither philosophical nor moral commit-ments have been behind it all.

I started selling seeds and mowing lawns simply because I liked bowling-alley milkshakes and onion rings, and tickets to the adjoining moviehouse. And my allowance was never, ever going to pay for those things.

What drives me today? Well, I limit milkshakes to one or two a year, and I don't need a budget for onion rings or movie tickets. Now it's just the enjoyment of being mildly busy and creative. Knowing that the things I do make others happy, or improve life in some way. Doing the things my hand finds to do.

I have been exceedingly blessed that someone has always found my skills valuable. For that I am grateful.

And for this new season which I am entering? I'm excited.

Wonderstuck, even.

∎

Panang

Misuk met my secret lover, Panang, over lunch in Wenatchee yesterday. It was a threesome.

A foursome, really, but Pad Thai doesn't count. No love affair there. But have you ever had a really good Panang curry?

I was first exposed to Thai food during my days as a lowly software engineer at Quinton Instrument Company in Seattle. At the time, the company was housed in a massive concrete-and-steel bunker on Denny Way, and there were a good number of decent lunch destinations within short walking distance.

One of these was a largish Thai restaurant run in connection with a local hotel. I don't know if I ever even knew the name of the hotel... but the restaurant was Thai Palace, and it was the default choice of the Quinton Engineering Department for Friday lunches.

In my early twenties, I was not given to such outlandish cuisine. At that point, my palate was constrained to what one might find at a Skipper's, a Pizza Haven, a Red Robin, a Casa Lupita, or in a Betty Crocker cookbook. I was not what one would call culinarily adventurous, so I long resisted the Friday lunch outings.

When I did start joining the crew, I stuck to obvious-looking dishes like the Pad Thai or the Pad See Ew. But when I heard orgasmic sounds coming from one of my fellow engineers and saw what he was eating... well, I was intrigued. (The gentleman in question may, in fact, have been Cliff Curry; I do not recall.)

That my first exposure to curry in general was a Panang curry meant that all other curries would be something of a letdown. The Panang is a curry specific to a particular town in Thailand, and the combination of spices involved is both unique and difficult to replicate if one is not from that area or trained in the specifics of the curry's preparation. The distinctive flavor is derived from, among other things including the actual curry, Thai basil, kaffir lime, bell pepper, and coconut milk. And I have been in love with Panang curry from my very first bite.

I enjoyed the Thai Palace Panang, which was prepared with a choice of protein but was probably best with white chicken meat, probably hundreds of times; years later, after Thai Palace closed (as all good things must come to an end), my friend the Shy Pilot and I discovered Emerald Thai in an ancient log-cabin restaurant on Pacific Highway in Des Moines. This joint was run by a family that actually hailed from the area around Panang, and they were so amused by our repeated (and laser-focused) enthusiasm for their Panang curry that the hostess would have the chef prepare extra sauce for the Shy Pilot to take home and, ahem, drink.

But alas! After many years, Pac Hiway was renamed International Boulevard, the neighborhood and demographics changed, and Emerald Thai closed its doors. Not long after, my late wife, Jenn, passed away, and I moved from Des Moines to the Methow. And there is no Thai here. Imitations? Yes, from time to time on certain menus, but certainly nothing like a real Panang. These days, I get the odd sample at sporadic visits to Seattle or Bend, Oregon. But it has been literally years since I had a first-rate Panang.

And then... yesterday.

Ah.

Wenatchee, Washington, features a Thai restaurant simply called The Thai. To date, Misuk and I had been unable to enjoy a visit because they are closed between lunch and dinner hours, and due to various Covid interferences. For whatever reason, the several times we had tried to dine at The Thai, they simply were not open.

Ah, but yesterday we were in Wentachee on business and made a point of being sure to arrive before The Thai closed following lunch.

And the Panang. Oh, my. With just the first bite I was in heaven. It was like being back at Thai Palace again, in 1986. It made me feel young again... not that I feel particularly old on the brink of sixty, but I think you know what I mean.

Misuk believes that a happy soul begins with good food (garbage in, garbage out, as they once said in software circles), and I must say I agree. I have eaten better since getting together with Misuk than I have in my entire life. There are probably reasons other than genetics that Asian people tend to look and feel so good as they age!

Happy mouth and happy gut = happy wife and happy life.

But seriously… if you are ever in Wenatchee and happen to be around when The Thai is open, you might consider a taste of the Panang curry.

I, for one, have been wonderstruck.

∎

Loose Change

Glasgow is where I started finding money.

In December 2002, my late wife, Jenn, and I were on a three-week sabbatical in Europe. After a week at a remote Highlands refurbished stables-turned-B&B, we had a laundry day in Glasgow.

Now, "launderettes" are not what we are used to in the United States. In the UK, you typically have two options for doing laundry. If you launder at home, you have a combo washer/dryer (read: washer/damper); it just wrings things out as much as it can, and then after some pointless and lengthy tumbling, you end up taking things out and line-drying them, draping them over furniture, or (if it's winter) propping things in front of heat registers, fireplaces, and towel bars. If you patronize a launderette, though, it's more like laundering at a dry-cleaner's here in the States: You drop off your bag and come back hours later for your completed loads.

Jenn and I opted for the latter, since we were holed up at a Holiday Inn for the night before flying out to Budapest; and as we were milling about the shops adjacent to George Square, we started talking about little games we could play with each other during the remainder of our time in Europe.

"I know!" Jenn said with excitement. "We could see who finds the most loose change on the street, like Daddy and I used to do during our walks!"

This sounded exactly like a losing proposition to me. "I don't think so," I objected. "In my family, Bob's the one who finds money. I'm the one who doesn't."

One of my earliest memories of my brother is from the summer I was four years old in Missouri. We lived in a trailer court near the county fairgrounds in Sedalia, and as the family was walking over the hill through the tall grass one day Bob found several dollars in bills and change. And not just in one place, the way I remember it. He picked up loot in three or four different places! The rest of us? Zilch.

It was always like that with Bob. He was like a money magnet. And I was like money repellent. Even when I earned money it vanished quickly. (The lone exception was when I did a seat belt repair in the back seat of my dad's beater 1962 Impala, which had apparently been a taxicab in a former incarnation. That was a veritable trove of silver coinage.)

Bob, meanwhile, was always building bank accounts and acquiring real property.

So this became part of my identity: "The Guy Who Doesn't Find Money." I reminded Jenn of that fact.

Jenn chided me. "Greg, you are the one who's always telling me that my language creates my reality and that if I want different results I need different self-talk."

She had me, but I still resisted. "So you're telling me that if I say, 'I am the guy who finds money,' that I'll actually start finding money?" Jenn just kind of smirked, knowing that my question was both defensive and semi-rhetorical.

So for the next three hours, as we waited for our scheduled return to the launderette, we simply walked the streets of Glasgow. And as I repeatedly muttered under my breath, "I am the guy who finds money!" I, in fact, did. We both did. Over the next two weeks we found dozens of coins.

And we never stopped. Starting in 2003, we kept annual tallies of the values of coins and bills we each found, and various bonuses were awarded from the household budget for "Shiniest Coin," "Most Unrecognizable Coin," "Most Unusual Coin," "Best Foreign Coin," and the like. Oh, and "Highest Dollar Value," which I often won.

Other memorable finds over the years include a dime I spotted on a crosswalk island at a Burien freeway exit on Jenn's birthday and which I circled back just to retrieve in her honor. She also couldn't believe the nickel I spotted in the moonlight from the living room of our third-floor apartment. I was certain the glimmer by the drain grate in the parking lot below was a coin, and Jenn thought I was crazy. I dashed out in my bare feet in the rain just to prove her wrong.

And then there was the time we raided the trash heaps at an airport auto detailing shop… because, you know, taxicabs. And loose change. Jackpot!

And because… *I am a guy who finds money*.

Truly, you find what you seek. Forty years of one identity, twenty years of another.

Clarity

Have I mentioned that I am a word nerd?

Allow me to—ahem!—clarify a few things.

At the University of Washington, my nerdity led me to study closely with Associate Professor Míceál Vaughn, who at the time was producing an electronically searchable Middle English text of the *Piers Plowman A* manuscript. (Vaughn's work on this text was finally published in 2011.) I can't remember if I received credit or payment for my work on this project, but during my final months as an undergraduate I would spend hours at a time in the brand-new English Department computer lab hunched over a facsimile of the text, transcribing sequences of specialized character codes onto floppy disc files utilizing a bank of Kaypro micro-computers.

Yes, this was the early 1980s.

As a result, I became pretty facile with reading Middle English texts in the original Blackletter script. Fast forward a couple decades and my Kindlings Muse Podcast colleague Jennie Spohr turned me on to a facsimile edition of the Tyndale Bible. Originally published in 1526, the Tyndale predated the King James... but was still essentially the King's English which appeared in the "authorized English version" of 1611 and which remains widely in print today. The newly published Tyndale facsimile edition, however, about which Jennie raved, presented the text in all its original Blackletter-on-parchment illuminated glory.

Have I also mentioned that I am an ordained pastor?

The sheer joy with which I took my time reading through the Tyndale, over a year or so, cannot be expressed. Word nerd meets pastor meets historical text. Ahhhh…

My appetite had been whet… and I went in search of other facsimile manuscripts. To my utter joy, I discovered that a facsimile edition of the 1388 Wycliffe Bible existed! Contemporary with Chaucer's penning of his bawdy *Canterbury Tales* for the royal court, John Wycliffe and his cohort were clandestinely risking their lives to produce the first common-English translation of the Christian Scriptures.

Wycliffe and many of his aides would pay for this work with their lives, as at the time the Catholic Church held a stranglehold on Latin masses. Anything else was dangerously heretical.

But a handful of Wycliffe's Bibles survived the purge, and one copy has been scanned for study at universities and made available as a PDF on CD-ROM. By the time I discovered its academic existence, however, the company who published the PDF (along with other medieval texts) had gone out of business. The Internet, naturally, had rendered distribution of CD-ROMs commercially unviable.

Through some diligent Internet sleuthing, I nonetheless managed to find an actual number for an actual telephone that an actual person actually answered, literally just hours before the last crates of CD-ROMs were being sent to the dump. Not long after, my copy of the Wycliffe Bible PDF facsimile arrived in the mail.

My tour through this edition of the biblical text has been much more leisurely than my read of the Tyndale. The Wycliffe is true Middle English, which, though I can read quite well, nonetheless requires a good deal of reflection and slow study. The language is not what it used to be in the 14th century, and I do frequently have to resort to online helps to decipher the Blackletter minims or come up with a definition for a certain word. English was in great flux at the time and was sprinkled with many French and Dutch influences.

Did I mention that I wished to clarify a few things?

Well, here is my point today.

While making my way through Jesus' "Farewell Discourse" in chapters 13-17 of the Gospel of John, I came across what, to me, was a fairly startling word usage.

In modern language, we would "read" Wycliffe's translation of John 13:31-32 as,

> Jesus said, Now man's Son is glorified, and in him and through him, God is glorified. If God is glorified in him, then God shall glorify him in himself, and he shall glorify him now.

What Wycliffe actually wrote, however, was:

> Jesus said, Now man's Son is clarified, and God is clarified in him. If God is clarified in him, and God shall clarify him in himself, and anon he shall clarify him.

In short, our modern words "glorify" and "clarify" have the same root. Two or three times throughout the Farewell Discourse, Wycliffe opts for "glorify"... but for the vast majority of the dozens of usages, "clarify" is the word of choice.

For this word nerd and pastor, the discovery has been kind of Earth-shattering. Though raised in the church, immersed in its "Christianese," and formally schooled in its theology and scriptures, I have never really understood what this whole notion of "glorification" is about.

Now, in contemporary parlance I certainly understand what "glorification of violence" means and what unwarranted glorification of celebrities like Aaron Rodgers means.

But when we sing "Glorify thy name" during church worship services, I have been at a loss. What the heck does that even mean? If I want to glorify something, what is it *that I actually do?* In practice, it seems, glorification means talking a good game without actually getting on the playing field. It means paying lip service to God and waving our hands on Sunday mornings while going about our own private business the rest of the day, and the rest of the week.

In other contexts, we certainly understand what it means to *worship*. Somebody who worships wealth, for instance, spends every waking hour pursuing and accumulating wealth. No days off. A single-minded obsession. Ebenezer Scrooge, for instance. Somebody who worships celebrity tweets tirelessly, constantly maintaining a high profile on social media. No days off. A focused strategy. Say, Kim Kardashian.

Worshiping God, though? We have turned it into a mostly spare-time endeavor, squeezed in between trips to the supermarket, work days, vacations, and perhaps holidays. It starts at 10:00 AM and by God better be over by 11:30. Because we are not *clear in our minds* about who He is and why He is to be worshiped—much less how, where, and when.

But Wycliffe... well, he gets it right. There's *clarity*. When God "glorifies" Jesus, He says, "This is my beloved Son, in whom I am well pleased. He's the one. He's the Messiah. Listen to Him. If you want to know Me and what I value, look at Jesus, and see what He values. Have I made Myself clear?" It's an identity thing.

When Jesus glorifies God, He says, "This is my Father. I see what He does, and that's what I do, too. He's the one. He is Lord. Listen to Him. If you have seen Me, you have seen Him. Have I made Myself clear?" It's an identity thing.

For four chapters of John's text, Jesus clarifies a great deal about Himself, about his Father, and about the Spirit. And when we are *clear in our minds* about these things, that's when the idea of "glory" starts to make more sense... at least to me.

The Greek word which Wycliffe translated as "clarify" and which we today translate as "glorify" is *doksázō*, meaning "valuing one for one's actual self." And to value God for Himself, we have to be clear about who He is. To value Christ for Himself, we have to be clear about who He is. To value the Spirit for Itself, we have to be clear about who the Spirit is. If we are not clear about these things, we cannot value the Father, the Son, and the Spirit properly.

And finally, we have to be *clear about who we are* and who we are not.

So I am now clear in my mind: Glorification of the Trinity is not some vague waving of arms, uplifted palms, or a decidedly part-time "worship" based in personal convenience. Glorification is, in fact, a real understanding of the powers of this universe and a willingness to yield to those powers—and to all the good that they want for us, rather than to a deadly pursuit of our own agendas and passions. Because, as Paul writes in Ephesians 3, these powers want more for us than all we can ask or imagine.

From *doksázō* we also get the "Doxology," penned in 1709:

> Praise God from whom all blessings flow;
> Praise him, all creatures here below;
> Praise him above, ye heavenly host:
> Praise Father, Son, and Holy Ghost.

Because they have been clarified.

■

Boonie

I wasn't supposed to be in Torrey, Utah, on the morning of October 11, 1998.

I have written before of the otherworldly encounter my late wife and I had with Boone Johnston at Rainbow Christian Church and of the tremendous affirmation it was of our union.

When I attempted to contact him a year later, a woman at the church, now no longer called Rainbow Christian, told me that no one by the name Boonie Johnson had ever pastored the church. And there the mystery lay for sixteen years: a desert encounter with an angel (which simply means "messenger"), who appeared to no longer exist... The indelible impression persisted.

Over those years, I would periodically revisit my Internet search for Boonie. In 2015 I found him. The Internet finally caught up to him, and I got the best of my search engine results. He was indeed very real and not an angel.

Well, not *that* kind, anyway. Certainly a messenger!

The long years had landed him in a counseling ministry in Arizona. A phone call confirmed that this was indeed the same Boonie Johnson, and he confirmed my recollection of the events of October 11, 1998.

He also related to me the circumstances surrounding his "disappearance" from Torrey.

Boonie had been caring for his niece in Torrey, and just prior to her graduation from high school in 1999, he had resigned from his pastorate. Even though many of his parishioners—scattered across the several rural towns he served—had become aware he was gay and accepted him, he knew that his days at the Torrey church were numbered. The official response of the congregation, affiliated with the Southern Baptist Convention, was brutal. They set about literally canceling Boonie and the entire history of Rainbow Christian Church. It was a purge.

From Torrey, Boonie relocated to St. George, where his niece enrolled in college until transferring to Texas A&M to complete her degree. Boonie then moved to Arizona, where he began working with a counseling service that ministers to gay males and opened a business with his partner, Christopher, who passed away from a stroke in 2008. In October 2015, I caught up with Boonie just prior to his marriage to Andre LeBlanc.

Boonie LeBlanc is now retired and lives in Pinal County, where he continues to volunteer counseling hours, work with food banks and homeless shelters, and "spread the news that God loves and accepts people as they are."

I have been blessed by my long if sporadic friendship with Boonie and am proud to call him a fellow worker for Christ. He is no more perfect than am I, or you, of course, a fact that pastors generally come to eventually; nor is he any more worthy of the appellation "Christian," which means "little

Christ," than am I or you. But I can guarantee, and the evidence is there, that Boonie strives to represent the love of Christ well.

And oh, how the Spirit moves in him.

Been there, seen it, got the T-shirt. Wonderstruck.

■

Finding the Lost

"I've lost my glasses!" called a complete stranger from the middle of the Missouri River.

"I think I can help with that!" I called back.

At this point, my companions and I were several days into a week-long canoe trip on the "White Cliffs" section of the river in Montana, in the Upper Missouri River Breaks National Monument.

The river is fairly broad and shallow at the Eagle Creek campground, and the beach was full of empty canoes. Tents littered the treeline, sparse enough as it was, and in the 95-degree late-July heat the canoeists were mostly lounging near the water, while the braver (or more foolhardy) were actually *in* it.

Montana is cattle country, after all, and the Missouri River is sort of the region's sewage sluice. Cow pies often float whole in the water, which is mostly a thin brown soup. Swimming in the stuff risks ear and other infections.

Nonetheless, when you've been paddling all day in the sun you get awfully hot—and even thin brown soup can be tempting, as long as it's cold.

And so it was that my nephews and a great many other folks were frolicking in the waist-high wrack. I, however, resolutely stayed above the waterline.

After a while, though, I noticed a knot of people, about one hundred yards out, all milling about peering into the soup. Even where I was, I could tell that such an effort was fruitless—whatever it was they were looking for.

"What's up?" I hollered.

"I've lost my glasses!" called a complete stranger from the middle of the Missouri River.

"I think I can help with that!" I called back. And with that, I kicked off my moccasins and waded into the soup.

Now, although I have always been very dexterous with my feet, I probably should have been hesitant about offering my assistance. Finding a pair of glasses in the middle of the muddy Missouri is not unlike the proverbial search for a needle in a haystack... which, by the way, is a lot more easily accomplished in bare feet.

But here, I knew the river bed was hard-packed sand; and armed with an engineer's logic, and a good deal of cocky self-assurance, I figured my odds of success were well better than even.

"So where were you standing when you dropped your glasses?" I asked the woman when I reached the searchers.

"I really have to find them!" she exclaimed. "They're not sunglasses. They're my prescription glasses, and I'm nearly blind without them!"

"It's okay. Just show me where you were when you dropped them."

"Oh, but I didn't drop them!" She was breathless. "I put them on top of my head to wash my face, and when I bent over to scoop water, off they went!" She pointed to her left. "About here."

"Okay." I came alongside and gauged the direction of the current's drift. I peered down and confirmed the uselessness of trying to see anything, then lifted my eyes to the horizon.

And then I began to slowly and gingerly sidestep my way downstream. The current was strong enough to carry away any light debris, and all that my gingerly treading toes could feel was cool hardpack.

A very, very large cow pie drifted by.

And then, about fifteen feet downstream, my toes struck what I was looking for: an extended arm of the woman's eyeglasses. I wrapped my big and second toes around it and lifted the glasses above the water, balancing on my left foot. I wasn't about to put anything more than my feet and legs in that water!

"Here they are!" I declared. Less than a minute had passed, and the flabbergasted woman waded over to take her glasses from my extended foot.

As I said, I've always been very good with my feet.

But that was legendary.

A Hat

Is it possible to be wonderstruck by a hat?

Well, in my case, apparently so.

In late July of 1999, I rolled into Fort Benton at about 3:30 in the morning. At the end of a fourteen-hour drive from Seattle, I was treated to an amazing display of the Aurora Borealis as I was puzzling over the "lost time" I experienced somewhere on the back highways through the Rockies. I arrived almost an hour earlier than I should have been able to. I sometimes drive a little over the speed limit… but not that much!

To this day, I have not been able to figure out the details of that drive. I was on schedule as far as Butte… and then, in the darkness of a summer night, time went wonky. I was aware of being kind of woozy for a while and thinking that the taillights ahead of me seemed odd; I could never catch them up, but I also never fell behind, until I finally stopped for gas in Helena. And, by then, time had been broken.

And yes, I do know about time zones. That was not the issue. For whatever reason, I guess, I was just meant to see the Northern Lights that morning.

After I napped a bit and scavenged a breakfast, and before my Missouri River trip companions arrived to begin our week on the river, I visited the outfitter's shop. I had a good oilskin hat with me that I had worn on other expeditions… but I wanted something more appropriate for the heat and exposure of July Missouri River sun.

What I found was the ideal packable hat. It featured a lightweight semi-rigid Cordura bill that would survive washing when necessary, a long stiffish neck flap reminiscent of the French Foreign Legion, a universal elastic size adjustment that dangled from the back of the hat to secure the flap (when appropriate) and the Croakies attached to my sunglasses. And you could stuff the mustard-and-plum-colored hat into a back pocket, if need be, without fear of damaging it.

The hat was called a PakHat, manufactured by Lights of the Sky, Ltd. in Bozeman, the brainchild of Montana outdoors enthusiast Mary Cates. "PakHats are designed for people who want to live with the elements," said the tag on the hat, "not fight them." The label in my hat said it had been made in 1991. The slogan: *Adventure Ahead.*

I bought that hat, and it was indeed perfect for that week on the Missouri. And I wore it many, many other times. Other river trips. Weeks in Scotland. Countless days in the woods. I wore it so often that it eventually began to wear out.

When the first danger signs arose, probably ten years ago or more, I tried to find Mary Cates and Lights of the Sky… yes, *Lights of the Sky*, like the Aurora I saw the morning I bought the hat! But the phone number on the hat and those I found through Google all were dead. It seemed that Lights of the Sky had faded from the Earth… and that made me profoundly sad.

When holes finally appeared in the crown of the hat, on a backpacking trip while I was closing on my house in Twisp four years ago, I stopped washing it and then stopped using it altogether. For three years I tried wearing other hats… and during those years I started working at (and then ended up co-owning!) a hat store in Winthrop. So I knew what the options were and are… and none of them measured up to that PakHat. It was simply exceptional.

Two weeks ago, after putting my PakHat back in service for the summer season, I finally knuckled under and took it to a local seamstress for repair. And then went home and sulked. It might get reinforced, but it wouldn't be the same.

So I took to Google once again. This time, I came up with a Bozeman newspaper article, from nearly thirty years ago, that referenced both Mary… and her husband! Armed with *his* name, I had a new lead. And found a new phone number to try.

It worked. Mary picked up my message and called.

Now, today, more than twenty years later, I not only have a replacement for my mustard-and-plum PakHat from the very same 1991 lot… I have *dozens*. In a variety of colors and configurations. Including fleece for winter wear.

And I have them on the shelves at The Iron Horse in Winthrop. When I unpacked the shipment, I nearly peed myself. (I am nearly sixty, after all.)

I am so grateful that Mary warehoused these after she closed her business.

Gosh, but this is one strange and wonderful world!

■

Vivian

I only met Vivian La Francoeur once, at a summer camp some forty-five years ago.

Summer camps were generally not a good experience for me. In the first place, I was typically younger than everyone else at camp, just as I was at school, and word travels fast: If there was any bullying to be done (and there usually was) the youngest kid is often the target... and I often was. Further, my natural disposition was to be a loner, so I frequently ended up both isolated and bullied. Such things can easily happen, and go unchecked, when a hundred or so kids are left mostly unsupervised at places like summer camps.

The camp at which I met Vivian was an entirely different experience. For whatever reason, just twenty-five or so kids were in attendance that week, which suppressed the natural *Lord of the Flies* effect. The counselor-to-kid ratio was also unusually high.

The kids at camp that week were also extraordinarily nice. I had never met any of them before (which in my world was an advantage) and, even though a good number of them called the same church in Pasco home and could have formed a naturally exclusive clique, I nonetheless felt welcomed as one of their own.

I only remember a couple of their names. A girl named Amy was one… and her friend Vivian La Francoeur. I was a good speller, and Vivian's surname evoked the romance of American frontier places like Coeur d'Alene as well as the French explorers that had named many of those places: Cartier, Champlain, Marquette, and Joliet. So Vivian's name always stuck in my head.

Vivian was also tremendously kind and serious-minded… though "serious" isn't quite the right word for it. She struck me as deeply thoughtful at an age when kids are typically frivolous in their pursuits. Amy and the others were unusually thoughtful, too; but there was something different going on with Vivian. She made quite an impression on me over those six summer days.

Fast forward forty-five years or so.

The other day I was reading another frontier exploration journal, and the writer's mention of other French-Canadian trappers made me think again of that very unique name: Vivian La Francoeur.

Pretty randomly, I set down my Kindle and picked up my phone to Google Vivian's name. The odds that she would be findable after several decades were pretty slim; but if she were still using her birth surname in any way, it would be one that Google would be sure to find.

It was probably the easiest Google search in history.

Vivian doesn't show up on the Internet a lot, but her career as a United flight attendant does make her pretty visible. She was interviewed for United and Boeing promotional materials, for instance, at the time the final 747 rolled off the assembly line in 2017.

I also found a phone number for Vivian. Googled numbers usually don't work, as they are typically old listings for disconnected land lines. So I didn't immediately call. After all, what would I say? And why would she answer a call from an unknown number?

So I just thought, "Well, that's interesting," and that was that.

But the idea stuck in my head. Just a couple days earlier I had been reading about the retiring of a private 747 jet; and that coincidence niggled at me. Because, you know, I am not a great believer in "coincidence."

I also thought: "I really *do* have something to say to Vivian. And it might be an encouragement to her."

When I sat down at my computer a couple days later, the search page with Viv's results was still open on one of my Chrome tabs, and I caved quickly to the urge to dial. The call immediately went to voicemail, and after Vivian's brief greeting I left a short message.

"Hi, Vivian. My name is Greg Wright, and I met you once long ago at a summer camp, Pleasant Valley Christian Camp's high school camp, I think. I just wanted to thank you for being kind to me at a time in my life when I wasn't experiencing much kindness. Have a great day!" I did not leave my number as I did not want Vivian to think this was some kind of weird stalking thing. If she even picked up the message, she could find my number in the call log if she liked.

Well, Vivian *did* listen to my message, and she *did* find my number in her call log. She called back not long after.

She did remember that week at camp with Amy (Sanders) and the others. But what stood out to her was the timing of my call.

Vivian had been waiting for another call at the time and so pushed mine to voicemail when it came in, not recognizing the number. Against her usual judgment, while she continued to wait for that call, she then listened to what she supposed would be a spam voicemail. It was, she said, exactly the message she needed that morning, at just the time she was questioning her impulses toward kindness and thoughtful consideration of others. She needed to hear that she was appreciated.

When I told her in detail how she had struck me those many years ago, she expressed surprise that I could have gleaned so much of her character given that we were both so young at the time. I explained that I had always been a pretty observant kid. It helps, in some ways, to be a loner—and open to serendipity.

Not surprisingly, there is also significance in names.

La Francoeur means "The Open Heart."

Gregory means "Watchful."

Wonderstruck.

Coincidence?

Strategic thinking is second nature to me.

I suppose I could attribute that to my excellent training in management skills, but the fact remains that, since the time I graduated from college, well before my sojourn as a corporate project manager, my life has followed a pattern of well-defined five-year phases. I could bore you by trotting them out in list form, but I will not. Today, I only wish to talk about the five-year phase which has definitely come to a close as a new one begins.

Jason Suter, the pastor at Winthrop Friendship Alliance Church, asked me a few weeks ago to cover the sermon for him on April 16. At the time I accepted his invitation, I intended to speak about Philip and the Ethiopian eunuch from the book of Acts.

But then one Wednesday night at the Bible study I lead, only my wife, Misuk, and I were in attendance. The subject matter came from the Gospel of Mark, Jesus' encounter with a demon-possessed man in a Gerasene graveyard. That story follows the episode when a storm rages on the Sea of Galilee with Jesus asleep in the stern, a situation about which the disciples were not particularly pleased.

The conversation that Misuk and I shared that evening was profound and moving enough to rest in my brain and heart for days afterward. Eventually I thought, "No, these insights are important enough to share with the whole congregation." And I notified Jason of my intent to change topics.

So, you see, I wasn't supposed to be talking about Jesus and that storm on April 16.

And then again, I was.

Now, it so happened yesterday that I was searching through the archives on my blog for a piece to share at a poetry reading tonight... and in the process I came across the following, which I wrote *exactly five years ago*.

That I was entering a new five-year phase at the time is salient; that my thoughts should come so definitively full circle in five years time... well, you be the judge.

> There is only one rule of any real value, and it is this: That one must first demonstrate mastery of a rule before one may earn the right to break it.

My inventory of self-rediscovery continues. Change is afoot, and these are truths about who I am and what my life needs to look like:

1. First and foremost, right now, I need to live a life that values acted-out love above further learning.
2. I need to continue a life of spaciousness, leaving time for both God and people.
3. I need to live a life that gets me outdoors, often and meaningfully, so that I do not seek refuge in dreams.
4. I need to live a life that looks a lot more like a Spartan

ten-foot-square room than a house full of stuff I rarely use and wouldn't care if I never saw again; I need to further reject materialism.
5. I need to live a life that looks more and more like a servant than like a wage-earner.
6. NEW TODAY: I am a survivor. I fear pain less than I fear not doing what is right. This is a fact.
7. NEW TODAY: I am powerfully attuned to what God is doing in this world and in my life. I may forget this from time to time, but it is nonetheless true.
8. NEW TODAY: While the storm rages, Jesus is comfortably asleep in the back of the boat. (For you rafters out there, that's "on the Princess Pad.") And I'm good with that. The thought makes me smile.

I almost hyperventilated while reading Laurence Gonzales' *Deep Survival* this morning, much as I did while watching Todd Haynes' *Wonderstruck* on March 12.

Because of my guilt over returning my cats Grynne & Bearrett to MEOW feline rescue later today—because, as a bachelor again, I simply cannot pay adequate attention to two clingy cats—I deliberately planned the morning to be together with them one last time, even taking the daily 9:30 AM UPS delivery schedule into account so the girls wouldn't be disturbed while I read.

In an odd choice, I decided to include *Deep Survival* in my reading this morning. I don't know why. I guess because I was including "more time." So even though that's been my nightly reading material the last few weeks, and I hadn't done any in days, I picked it up on the way to the recliner.

First, I settled in with the girls. Then I napped, for a good long time. Then I read Romans 15, about how confident Paul is in his readers' ability to listen to God. Then I read James 5, about the letting go of possessions and about the need to be patient with what seeds have been sown.

Then I settled in to read what turned out to be the final chapter of *Deep Survival*, though I had no idea that was the case at the time. (The book concludes with a lengthy appendix, so I thought I had several chapters left, which was not the case. This is sooooo much like what happened with *Detectorists* in March... but that's also another story.)

About the time I got the sense that this *was* the final chapter, and that there were only a few pages left, G&B's ears perked up. The UPS van had arrived. But the girls did not leap down, as is their custom. And John, the driver, for whatever reason, did not yet come to the door. I guess he was getting his load organized.

The three of us were left alone to finish the chapter together. John did not come to the door until my breath had been taken away, until the crux of the conclusion had been passed—and I knew that God had spoken to me yet again with profound clarity.

I could quote endlessly from the final pages of that final chapter. But how I *felt* about it, what it *meant* to me, is summed up by this:

> Survival in the moment, or over hours or days or months, whether that survival comes about by chance or effort or an

inexplicable combination, must be followed once more by the same struggle that led to that point.

Speaking of his father, the author concludes,

> Catastrophe had not broken him. ... Adversity annealed him. It gave him endless energy. He taught me the first rule of survival: to believe that anything is possible.

Yeah. Struggle *does* follow survival. And I'm in. Believe it.

I am not really sure I've mastered my own First Rule, stated at the top of this note, but I saw this truth more clearly than I thought on Sunday, when I journaled that the Realm of Life

> ...is an unpredictable adventure
> Of moments stolen and found
> Of graffitied hearts in a river's midst
> Of cormorants preening in the sun
> Of plant profiles mingled with martyr's tales
> Of Waldo, located quite finally
> In a Mount Vernon dumpster.
>
> It is the open road traveled
> With an open mind and open eyes.
>
> Something wonderfully
> Mysterious.

■

Valerie

My mother, Valerie, used to have interests.

They were noticeable and definite. They occupied her thoughts and hours. She pursued them with vigor, often for years at a time.

She is eighty-seven years old now. After several years of medical complications, a heart attack and three stents, and a diagnosis of Alzheimer's disease, she has at last made a move this year into a retirement complex with managed care and memory care wings. Right now, she still lives independently with my father—but if you met her you'd never know that she ever had significant interests outside her marriage of nearly sixty-nine years. Aside from eating meals, the only thing she does with any regularity is watch *Wheel of Fortune*, *Jeopardy*, and episodes of *SVU*.

As a child, I would never have guessed that my mother would settle into a TV recliner for several hours a day at the end of her life. If anything, I would have imagined her falling asleep on a sofa with a book spread over her chest—or face, depending on how suddenly she would have nodded off.

My mother was an even more voracious reader than I have ever been—a good model for a young boy and eventual writer. She would settle into a hefty historical novel for hours at a time, often kept company by the family cat, Frisky. Authors on her bookshelf which I can remember without trying include Anya Seaton, Norah Lofts, Susan Howatch, and Jean Plaidy. I believe she also read the entire *Sharpe* series, which *Wikipedia* tells me was created by Bernard Cornwell.

Once in a while I would pick up something my mom would be reading and give it a go. Some of them were quite good. (I was more interested in my brother's hand-me-downs: Alistair MacLean, Leon Uris, J.R.R. Tolkien.) I know that I finished several of her books after she had done with them... and they weren't library books. My mom *bought* them.

Much of what I know of British and early American history came from discussions that my mother and sister, Elane, would have about what she was reading—books that would also include the journals of Lewis and Clark and *Andersonville*. My mom was both a fiction junkie and a history buff. Much of that rubbed off on me.

Mom also fully supported family forays, led by my father, into neighborhood cinemas. I know I saw (and was terrified by) *Bambi* when I was five, but my earliest movie memory is a double feature of *West Side Story* and *Duel at Diablo*. As I got a little older, the films of David Lean—*Doctor Zhivago, Lawrence of Arabia, Bridge on the River Kwai*—found their way into the rotation, along with films from classic 1970s auteurs like Sidney Lumet (*Dog Day Afternoon, Serpico, Prince of the City*), Alan J. Pakula (*The Parallax View, All the President's Men*), Sydney Pollack (*Three Days of the Condor, Jeremiah Johnson*), and William Friedkin (*The French Connection, Sorcerer*).

Take a look at those film titles. A diet of pretty serious cinema for a six- to twelve-year-old! And Mom wasn't just along for the ride, either. Sure, we went to see pop titles like *Chitty Chitty Bang Bang* and *Oliver!*, too. But my parents were very steady and serious consumers of cinematic art. Again, it's no accident that I also turned out to be a film critic and script consultant.

My mom was also instrumental in organizing annual family outings to the Seattle Symphony and productions of the Seattle Gilbert and Sullivan Society—which generally expanded into social occasions with family friends. She was my dad's partner at monthly Bridge games—for decades. She was quite serious about difficult paint-by-numbers projects; crochet and latch-hook; innovative and economical holiday decorations; cross-stitch embroidery; sewing. As the 1970s progressed she even became a fan of Queen! When my folks started sleeping on a hide-a-bed in the adjoining rec room while my grandmother convalesced in the master bedroom upstairs, she would ask me to play side B of *A Night at the Opera* at bedtime. *Figaro! Magnifico!*

Outside the house, she thoroughly enjoyed camping and hunting trips, gardening, suntanning, and beach-combing. When she was fifty-six she rafted the Grand Canyon. As she and Dad aged, she became an avid ocean cruiser—particularly in search of beaches and sun.

She collected shells, and she collected rocks.

And it is this latter enthusiasm that provoked this recollection of my mother's interests.

Mom collected rocks from all over the United States and the Caribbean. She traveled extensively and was always on the lookout for interesting stones.

Most of them were on the small side and of the sort which looked fabulous when wet—eye-catching baubles in the surf or stream. But back at home, they would lose their luster... yet Mom would not desert them. For her, they were memories.

One year for Christmas, Dad gave Mom a rock tumbler to, *ahem!*, polish up a quart or so of her favorite stones. Into the tumbler they went... and out came sand. Mom was crushed. But it did not deter her from collecting more stones.

Some of Mom's rocks, though, were on the larger side—as big as your fist. These she would line along the windowsills at their beach-front retirement chateau on Maplewild Drive in Burien. When they moved to Huntington Park in Des Moines, these were relocated to the deck railing.

A couple of months ago when I helped clean up the property in preparation for sale, I found one of her favorites—an angular chunk of red and purplish chert, from Arizona, I believe—ignominiously incorporated into a flowerbed border long-ignored and mossy.

There, it seemed to me, was a fitting symbol of my mother's loss of almost everything that once held her interest.

When they moved this most recent time, she asked for almost nothing to be taken with her. Things she has moved countless times—family heirlooms and photo collections; cherished books; her red, blue, and green antique glass collections; her sea shells; her stones—all abandoned like Woody and the gang in *Toy Story*.

Is this what growing up finally looks like? Or is it growing *out*? Outstripping all the things that once held your interest?

On one hand, I'd like to attribute the effect to Alzheimer's. What good are mementos if they remind you of... of... what was it? Things you no longer remember.

But I really don't think that's entirely it. Because I see that loss of interests in my father, too, and in many people as they age.

In Mom's case, I think the flagging of her interests coincided with Dad's retirement. For a few years, she held on to her weekly volunteering at Highline Hospital—but as their cruise schedule picked up and the two of them were spending more and more time together, everything else faded away. If the two of them couldn't enjoy something together, that something no longer happened. And rather than dive into a cross-stitch—as she might have done in years past when my dad was traveling, at work, or tied up with church business— she would turn on the TV as she would wait for my dad to fiddle his way through meeting minutes or emails. So they could be together some more when he was ready. Watching TV or playing cards. And now they don't even play cards.

All of her interests were, in a way, a means of filling up the time until Dad came home. All she ever really wanted was to spend time with him.

I think of that, now, as I approach the threshold of retirement age—and while I find myself pursuing new interests all the time, the pressures of retail push my wife and me more and more into time together at home. Everything else of a social nature seems so exhausting!

It makes me wonder: What will I be like at seventy or eighty years of age? Will I still be interested in publishing books, in writing poetry, in finding creative ways of managing to be out in the woods? Will Misuk and I still make a point of scheduling time away from each other to make room for literature and pickleball? And other people?

Or will we just settle into a routine of *Wheel of Fortune*? Or *Jeopardy*?

Who will be hosting then, do you think?

∎

Acknowledgements

There is no timeline for grief, but for me the two years following Jenn's tragic and magical passing were the crucible. I am indebted to those who were closest to me throughout my renaissance of joy:

- My oldest friend, Stephanie Cortes, always a trusted companion, who helped talk me through Jenn's hospice decline and beyond;
- My sister, Elane Rosok, who has always understood me, even when she tormented me as a child;
- Peter Alford, whose own life was in great flux as he encountered the closing months of mine and Jenn's, and who talked long and weekly with me for many years following Jenn's death;
- Fellow high school alumnus Denise Driscoll, who re-entered my life at just the right time to help get both my physical and spiritual bodies back in shape;
- College roommate John Adami, who has always seemed to have his forefinger on my spiritual pulse and re-enter my life at just the right times;

- Kaileah Akker, whose youthful energy and spiritual sensitivity has been invaluable in my journey on the eastern slope of the Cascades;
- Subhaga Crystal Bacon, whose friendship has encouraged a six-year outpouring of poetry and prose, and provided the final nudge to collect these essays;
- and most of all, my wife Misuk Ko, whose keen questions and close reading of my essays have taught me that I do not need to say (or write) everything that passes through my mind… just the stuff that really matters.

www.ingramcontent.com/pod-product-compliance
Lightning Source LLC
Chambersburg PA
CBHW032035150426
43194CB00006B/285